*$\mathcal{D}$ear Friends of* MAGNIFICAT,

*The book you now hold in your hands is a treasury of teachings, prayers, meditations, and witnesses from the saints to help guide you in one of the most beautiful and elevated devotions of the Catholic faith: Adoration of the Blessed Sacrament. In the Blessed Sacrament, the Most Holy Eucharist, we adore Christ himself. We are not faced with a mere symbol, but the true and substantial presence of our Savior—seen only with the eyes of faith, yes, but faith "is certain. It is more certain than all human knowledge because it is founded on the very word of God who cannot lie" (CCC 157). If ever you fear, even for the slightest moment, that God does not remain with you, that somehow you are all alone in this world, you have only to look towards the tabernacle, and the small flame that signals what lies within it, to be assured of the presence of God.*

*As you read and pray with this companion, may you grow in the certainty of Christ's love for you—for he is our ultimate Companion, our truest Friend, our one and only Savior. May you be confirmed in your joys, encouraged in your sorrows, and strengthened in the midst of temptations. May you one day join all those who see God face to face, who live and feast forever in the banquet of the King.*

*In the Eucharistic Heart of our Lord,*

Fr. Sebastian White, O.P.

# Table of Contents

# What Is Adoration?

The Benedictine Sisters
of Sacré Cœur de Montmartre

ADORATION IS DUE TO GOD ALONE. To adore the thrice-holy and supremely lovable God in the Blessed Sacrament exposed on the altar means that we offer ourselves to the ineffable love of God who has begun to manifest himself in creation, who has been revealed to us since Abraham, who has laid in Jesus Christ the foundation of the Church through which he acts in the world.

To pray before the Blessed Sacrament exposed on the altar is to cast a glance of faith upon Jesus Christ, true God and true man, truly present in the Bread of the Eucharist.

This prayer of adoration manifests God's mercy and tenderness for humanity and calls each one of us to intercede for the needs of men. *God so loved the world that he gave his only Son.* Jesus, the source of salvation, is offered for our contemplation and adoration incessantly. From him, all who pray to him receive an abundance of grace to live in this world as *beloved children*; and through him, in the Spirit, each of us returns to the Father, the God of tenderness and mercy, to bless and glorify him. Moreover, regardless of our poverty or wealth, through prayer, we can draw from the unfathomable riches of the Heart of Christ, given to us in the Eucharist, for the good of all people. Let us ask the Lord to make us worshipers *in spirit and truth,* witnesses of the love of God before the men and women of our time.

## The Treasury of God's Mercy

There is one action whose effect is boundless: it is our confident and insistent prayer. Even the poorest of believers, when he does not have much to give, still has an unknown wealth: to draw through prayer from the infinite treasury of God's mercy.

In the Gospel, the Lord calls us to perseverance in prayer. *Pray without ceasing. Watch and pray.* While our world lacks hope, a powerful remedy is offered to us. In a society that suffers from loneliness and individualism, Eucharistic adoration helps us discover the Real Presence of Christ at our side: *I am with you always, until the end of the age.* His love for us does not change. From him alone comes the stability of our life. The prayer of adoration allows us to welcome this love, to take this time of reflection in silence, to root ourselves in Christ and to allow our inner freedom to grow. Furthermore, Eucharistic adoration has the power to transform our everyday relationships by giving them the true meaning of human love.

Let us rediscover our sense of the beauty of the sacred. Let us habituate our gaze to receive in adoration the pure light of the Lord. Patiently, let us allow him to fashion, in the Holy Spirit, our true face, in his image and likeness, until the day of our eternal face-to-face: *Whoever has seen me has seen the Father.* And in the Communion of Saints, let us find all those whom we have loved and who have preceded us before him.

In the prayer of adoration, it is not a question, like the hypocritical Pharisee of the Gospel, of giving thanks for our own righteousness, and of praying only for others who are sinners (cf. Lk 18:9-14). But before the infinite love of God, given for us in Jesus, exposed before our eyes in the Blessed Sacrament, it is a question of recognizing ourselves as poor and sinful, to see that without him we can do nothing (cf. Jn 15:5), to let ourselves be saved by him, to let ourselves be healed, to let ourselves be converted. It is a question of offering ourselves to God the Father in the one and perfect offering of Jesus his Son, under the movement of the Holy Spirit, in order to fully accomplish his will. In this way, our prayer will be true: it will transform us, and in the Communion of Saints, it will shine forth as the grace of salvation for many men and women of our time who do not know God, who have distanced themselves from him, or who refuse his love.

*The Basilica of Sacré Coeur de Montmartre has been the site of continuous perpetual adoration of the Blessed Sacrament in Paris since 1885.*

# HISTORY AND FORMS OF EUCHARISTIC ADORATION

*The Eucharist is a priceless treasure: by not only celebrating it but also by praying before it outside of Mass, we are enabled to make contact with the very wellspring of grace.... It is pleasant to spend time with [Jesus], to lie close to his breast like the Beloved Disciple (cf. Jn 13:25) and to feel the infinite love present in his heart.*

– Saint John Paul II, *Ecclesia de Eucharistia*, 25

## Historical Background

The practice of reserving the Eucharist is an ancient observance which has its origins in the earliest centuries of the Church's history. The first extant description of reserving the Eucharist in order to bring Holy Communion to the sick is found in Saint Justin Martyr's First Apology (c. 155–157). During the following century, Saint Cyprian of Carthage described how Christians would bring the Eucharist to their homes to receive it during the week, since the celebration of the Eucharist usually took place only on Sundays at this point in Christian history. In a tradition beginning in the city of Rome, the Eucharist was sometimes reserved and then added to the Precious Blood during a later Mass celebrated in another location as a way of symbolically expressing the communion between parishes and their bishop or between various bishops. At other times, the reserved Sacrament from one Mass was added to the Precious Blood at a later Mass to signify the unity of all Eucharistic celebrations in Christ's Sacrifice on the Cross. In order to make the Eucharist available for these various purposes, the Blessed Sacrament was regularly reserved in tabernacles from the fourth century onward.

The common practice of praying before the reserved Eucharist began roughly in the eleventh and twelfth centuries as a consequence of the writings of certain Scholastic theologians on the subject of the Real Presence of Christ in the Eucharist. During this period, the dogma of transubstantiation, which is listed among the articles of faith, was first articulated. Transubstantiation is the term used by the Church to describe "the way in which Christ becomes present in [the Holy Eucharist] through the conversion of the whole substance of the bread into his Body and of the whole substance of the wine into his Blood." This teaching was formally defined by the Fourth Lateran Council (1215) and confirmed by the Council of Trent in 1551. At the time, the Council Fathers of Trent also reiterated the teaching of the Council of Constance (1415) concerning the doctrine of concomitance, which states that "Christ is present whole and entire in each of the [Eucharistic] species and whole and entire in each of their parts, in such a way that the breaking of the bread does not divide Christ."

As the faithful during the late Middle Ages meditated on the nature of Christ's Real Presence in the Eucharist, practices such as gazing upon the Eucharist at the time of the elevation of the host and chalice after the consecration at Mass, adoring the exposed Blessed Sacrament in the monstrance outside of Mass, and carrying the Eucharist in procession began to develop. At this time and during the centuries which followed, these rites were considered to be primarily devotional in nature, meaning that they were regarded as extensions of the Church's liturgical celebration of the Mass.

More recently, the Fathers of the Second Vatican Council reaffirmed the traditional teaching of the Church concerning the Real Presence of Christ in the Holy Eucharist. They taught:

> At the Last Supper, on the night when he was betrayed, our Savior instituted the Eucharistic Sacrifice of his Body and Blood. He did this in order to perpetuate the Sacrifice of the Cross throughout the centuries until he should come again, and so to entrust to his beloved Spouse, the Church, a memorial of his Death and Resurrection: a sacrament of love, a sign of unity, a bond of charity, a paschal banquet in which Christ is eaten, the mind is filled with grace, and a pledge of future glory is given to us.

During the Council, Saint Paul VI expressed his hope that the reform and restoration of the Mass called for by the Conciliar Fathers would "produce abundant fruits in the form of Eucharistic devotion, so that the Holy Church may, with this salvific sign of piety raised on high, make daily progress toward the full achievement of unity." In 1967, the Sacred Congregation of

Rites similarly emphasized the relationship between adoration of the Blessed Sacrament and the celebration of the Mass, indicating that "when the faithful adore Christ present in the sacrament, they should remember that this presence derives from the sacrifice and is directed toward both sacramental and spiritual Communion." The intimate connection between Eucharistic adoration and the celebration of Mass was more fully articulated and developed in *Holy Communion and Worship of the Eucharist Outside Mass* (1973). This document presents the worship of the Eucharist outside of Mass within the context of the official liturgical rites of the Church, noting that the Eucharist is "reserved after Mass to extend the grace of the sacrifice" of the Eucharistic celebration. This ritual book continues to guide the Church in her liturgical celebrations of offering worship to the Eucharist outside of Mass.

## Purposes of Eucharistic Worship Outside of Mass

The popes of our time have consistently encouraged the practice of worshiping the Eucharist outside of Mass. For example, in his annual Holy Thursday letter to priests in 1980, Saint John Paul II wrote that "the Church and the world have great need of Eucharistic adoration. Jesus waits for us in this sacrament of love. Let us be generous with our time in going to meet him in adoration and contemplation full of faith. And let us be ready to make reparation for the great faults and crimes of the world. May our adoration never cease."

In his 2005 Christmas address to the Roman Curia, Pope Benedict XVI similarly noted the value of adoring the Blessed Sacrament outside of Mass, saying, "only in adoration can a profound and genuine reception mature. And it is precisely this personal encounter with the Lord that then strengthens the social mission contained in the Eucharist, which seeks to break down not only the walls that separate the Lord and ourselves, but also and especially the walls that separate us from one another." More recently, Pope Francis has also reflected on how "one cannot know the Lord without the habit of adoring, of adoring in silence."

These papal statements and the historical development of Eucharistic adoration indicate that there are three purposes for the worship of the Eucharist outside of Mass:

- "to acknowledge Christ's marvelous presence in the sacrament";
- to lead to a fuller participation in the celebration of the Mass, culminating in the reception of Holy Communion; and
- to encourage and foster "worship which is due to Christ in spirit and truth."

## Eucharistic Adoration and Exposition

The worship and adoration of the Eucharist outside of Mass most often takes place when the Blessed Sacrament is reserved in the tabernacle. These times of private adoration and prayer offer the faithful a privileged opportunity to "easily, fruitfully, and constantly honor the Lord, present in the sacrament, through personal worship."

In addition to the private adoration of the Eucharist in the tabernacle, the Blessed Sacrament may be exposed in a monstrance or ciborium for display to the faithful. The exposition of the Blessed Sacrament is a public liturgical rite which is celebrated by the church community. Thus, the times of exposition should be scheduled when a sufficient number of the faithful can be present to pray before the exposed Eucharist. At no time should the Blessed Sacrament be exposed without anyone present.

Many parishes arrange at least annually for the solemn exposition and adoration of the Blessed Sacrament. This may take place within the context of a "Forty Hours" devotion or for some shorter period. Parishes may also schedule briefer periods of exposition more often throughout the year. Some religious communities and other groups, such as pious associations of the laity, have the practice of adoring the exposed Blessed Sacrament perpetually or for extended periods of time. When permission has been given for perpetual exposition of the Blessed Sacrament to take place in a parish church, this normally occurs in a chapel that is set apart and distinct from the body of the church so that liturgical services and other daily activities may take place in the church without interruption.

The Liturgy of the Hours may be celebrated in the presence of the exposed Blessed Sacrament. And the Congregation for Divine Worship and Discipline of the Sacraments has stated that the rosary, as "a prayer inspired by the Gospel and centered on the mystery of the Incarnation and the Redemption, 'should be considered a prayer of deep Christological orientation,' and may rightly be counted among the prayers designed to 'direct the attention of the faithful to the worship of Christ the Lord'" within the context of adoration of the exposed Blessed Sacrament.

Finally, the tradition of carrying the Eucharist in procession, especially on the Solemnity of the Most Holy Body and Blood of Christ (*Corpus Christi*), is encouraged by the Church's liturgical books. The purpose of such processions through the streets is to give public witness to the faith of the Christian people and to manifest their devotion to the Blessed Sacrament.

The Second Vatican Council reminded the Church that the Eucharistic Sacrifice is the summit and source of the Christian life. Inspired by this teaching, may our worship of the Lord's Body and Blood in the Most Holy Eucharist help us to experience the salvation Christ won for us and the peace of his kingdom.

– FATHER MATTHEW S. ERNEST

Father Ernest is the director of the Office of Liturgy for the Archdiocese of New York and professor of liturgy at Saint Joseph's Seminary (Dunwoodie). He holds a Doctorate of Sacred Theology from The Catholic University of America, Washington, D.C.

# WORDS OF COUNSEL AS YOU BEGIN TO ADORE

You have entered this chapel where you meet Jesus in his Eucharistic Presence. Now enter your heart, in the most intimate part of your being. Silence yourself. Silence all the voices that are in you, do not chase after useless thoughts. Your problems, your concerns, your anxieties, offer them to Jesus. During this time of worship, occupy yourself with him. Ask for the grace of abandonment and trust.

Put your eyes on Jesus in the Sacred Host. Begin to let your heart speak, that is, love him who loved us first. Pray not only with your lips, but also by meditating on the words you say. Choose a Psalm, a phrase from the Gospel, a simple little prayer, and repeat it silently, gently, and continually until it becomes your prayer, your cry, your supplication.

Enter in thanksgiving, in gratitude. Instead of considering only what you need or are lacking, give thanks for what you are and for what you have. Give thanks for what will be given to you tomorrow. You may experience fatigue or distraction, but take courage. As soon as you realize it, resume your prayer of the heart, gently. Ask the help of the Holy Spirit to help you in your weakness and to become your inner teacher.

Jesus wants to be at the center of your existence. Looking at him, learn, little by little, to go from "I" to "You"—from the desire to realize your projects to the desire for his will for you. He is solemnly exposed. Welcome the light that emanates from his Presence. As the sun warms and melts snow, he can continue to illuminate the darkness that envelops your heart until it is completely dispelled.

He hides under the simple and poor appearances of bread. He comes to you, poor, so that you may learn to welcome in truth your poverty and that of your brothers and sisters. You are in silence; remain in silence. Mary, *Stella Matutina* and *Porta Caeli*, Star of the Morning and Gate of Heaven, is with you on your way. She tells you the way and introduces you into the King's chamber. It is she who will make you understand, in silence, that by looking at Jesus you will discover the presence of the Blessed Trinity in you. And you will be able to experience in your life the words of Psalm 34: *Look to him and be radiant, and your faces may not blush for shame.*

⸻ ❁ ⸻

# Eucharistic Exposition and Benediction

*Once the people have assembled, a song such as the following may be sung while the priest or deacon prepares the Holy Eucharist for adoration.*

## O Saving Victim/O Salutaris Hostia

Meter: LM

O Saving Victim, op'ning wide
The gate of heav'n to us below!
Our foes press on from ev'ry side:
Your aid supply, your strength bestow.

*O salutáris hóstia,*
*Quae caeli pandis óstium:*
*Bella premunt hostília,*
*Da robur fer auxílium.*

To your great name be endless praise,
Immortal Godhead, One in Three;
O grant us endless length of days
When our true native land we see.

*Uni trinóque Dómino*
*Sit sempitérna glória:*
*Qui vitam sine término*
*Nobis donet in pátria.*

*The Liturgy of the Hours may be celebrated during the period of exposition, or there may be prayers, songs, readings from Scripture, and a brief homily to direct the attention of the faithful to the worship of the Lord.*

A reading from
the first Letter of Paul to the Corinthians          11:23-26

For I received from the
Lord what I also handed on

to you, that the Lord Jesus, on the night he was handed over, took bread, and after he had given thanks, broke it and said, "This is my body that is for you. Do this in remembrance of me." In the same way also the cup, after supper, saying, "This cup is the new covenant in my blood. Do this, as often as you drink it, in remembrance of me." For as often as you eat this bread and drink the cup, you proclaim the death of the Lord until he comes. The word of the Lord.

℟ **Thanks be to God.**

[Alternative Scripture readings begin on page 133].

*A Eucharistic song such as the following may be sung.*

### Come Adore/Tantum Ergo Sacramentum
Meter: 87 87 87

Come adore this wondrous presence,
Bow to Christ the source of grace.
Here is kept the ancient promise
Of God's earthly dwelling place.
Sight is blind before God's glory,
Faith alone may see his face.

> *Tantum ergo Sacraméntum*
> *Venerémur cérnui:*
> *Et antíquum documéntum*
> *Novo cedat rítui:*
> *Praestet fides suppleméntum*
> *Sénsuum deféctui.*

Glory be to God the Father,
Praise to his coequal Son,
Adoration to the Spirit,
Bond of love, in Godhead one.
Blest be God by all creation
Joyously while ages run.

*Genitóri Genitóque*
*Laus et jubilátio,*
*Salus, honor, virtus quoque*
*Sit et benedíctio:*
*Procedénti ab utróque*
*Compar sit laudátio.*

## BENEDICTION

*The priest or deacon may give a blessing. Before the blessing a prayer such as the following may be said.*

Minister: You have given them bread from heaven.

℟ Containing in itself all delight.

Minister: Let us pray.

O God, who in this wonderful Sacrament
have left us a memorial of your Passion,
grant us, we pray,
so to revere the sacred mysteries of your Body and Blood
that we may always experience in ourselves
the fruits of your redemption.
Who live and reign with God the Father
in the unity of the Holy Spirit,
one God, for ever and ever.

℟ Amen.

## The Divine Praises

Blessed be God.
Blessed be his Holy Name.
Blessed be Jesus Christ, true God and true Man.
Blessed be the Name of Jesus.
Blessed be his most Sacred Heart.
Blessed be his most Precious Blood.
Blessed be Jesus in the most Holy Sacrament of the Altar.
Blessed be the Holy Spirit, the Paraclete.

Blessed be the great Mother of God, Mary most holy.
Blessed be her holy and Immaculate Conception.
Blessed be her glorious Assumption.
Blessed be the name of Mary, Virgin and Mother.
Blessed be Saint Joseph, her most chaste spouse.
Blessed be God in his angels and in his saints.

### REPOSITION

*After the blessing the minister reposes the Blessed Sacrament in the tabernacle.*

*A closing song such as the following may be sung.*

### Holy God, We Praise Thy Name

* Repeat the last two lines.

> Holy God, we praise thy name!
> Lord of all, we bow before thee;
> All on earth thy scepter claim,
> All in heav'n above adore thee;
> Infinite thy vast domain,
> Everlasting is thy reign.*
>
> Hark! the loud celestial hymn
> Angel choirs above are raising;
> Cherubim and Seraphim
> In unceasing chorus praising,
> Fill the heav'ns with sweet accord:
> Holy, holy, holy Lord!*
>
> Holy Father, Holy Son,
> Holy Spirit, Three we name thee,
> While in essence only One,
> Undivided God we claim thee,
> And adoring bend the knee,
> While we own the mystery.*

# ADORATION OF THE BLESSED SACRAMENT AS A COUPLE

by Pierre-Marie Dumont

LOCAL CHURCHES OFFER OPPORTUNITIES FOR BELIEVERS to keep vigil before the Blessed Sacrament either in the tabernacle or exposed for adoration. The Eucharist is the source of Christian marriage. Spending time together before the Blessed Sacrament deepens the union of heart and soul in which the couple is joined through the Sacrament of Matrimony and plunged more profoundly through participation in the celebration of the Eucharist. You are invited to spend time in silence reflecting on the privilege of being there before Christ as one being in accord with the Father's will, adoring the sacrament of unity.

The following "hours" may be prayed at any time, but they are particularly appropriate during the public adoration of the Blessed Sacrament on Holy Thursday Evening, after the celebration of the Liturgy of the Lord's Supper—a celebration of the gift of the Eucharist, sacrament of love, to the Church, established by the One who loved his own to the end, as the couple is called to love one another to the end. It is a powerful opportunity to take into your communion as a couple your love for your children, your family, priests, the Church, all our brothers and sisters.

The "hour" need not last an entire hour, but it should include as much time as possible for silent prayer. If you can do so without disturbing others, you may want to pray parts of the "hour" aloud. One spouse could read the reading; both could read the meditation in silence, and, when the period of prayer is coming to an end, pray the prayer together.

## ■ FIRST HOUR ■

### *Jesus Institutes the Eucharist*

**Word of God**            Matthew 26:26-29

WHILE THEY WERE eating, Jesus took bread, said the blessing, broke it, and giving it to his disciples said, "Take and eat; this is my body." Then he took a cup, gave thanks, and gave it to them, saying, "Drink from it, all of you, for this is my blood of the covenant, which will be shed on behalf of many for the forgiveness of sins. I tell you, from now on I shall not drink this fruit of the vine until the day when I drink it with you new in the kingdom of my Father."

MEDITATION _____

### *The Eucharist Is the Very Source of Christian Marriage*

Christian spouses, live at the heart of the sacrament of covenant, your marriage nourished by the Eucharist and the Eucharist illuminated by your sacrament of marriage: the future of the world is at stake! At Mass, through the ministry of the priest, the Spirit of the Lord turns bread and wine into the body and blood of the Lord; in and through the sacrament of marriage, the Spirit can turn conjugal love into the very love of the Lord. Through the Lord's gift, human love can be totally irradiated by the source of love and can truly make manifest the new and eternal Covenant shining through it.

*SAINT JOHN PAUL II*

## PRAYER

God our Father,
you have called us each by name
and given us to one another in love.
You have granted us the grace
to be channels of your love to each other,
so that we may be for each other
the sacrament of your presence.

Give us the body of your Son,
through whom our union is made and sustained.
Give us the blood of your Son
who transfigures our love.

Day by day,
grant us the grace,
one through the other, one with the other,
   one in the other,
to make our love grow,
the love through which we will love you for ever
through Jesus Christ.

## ■ SECOND HOUR ■

### Prayer to Jesus for Unity in the Communion of Love

**Word of God**

John 13:33a, 34-35; 14:21; 15:9-10, 12-13; 17:1, 20-23

"MY CHILDREN, I will be with you only a little while longer. I give you a new commandment: love one another. As I have loved you, so you also should love one another. This is how all will know that you are my disciples, if you have love for one another.

"Whoever has my commandments and observes them is the one who loves me. And whoever loves me will be loved by my Father, and I will love him and reveal myself to him.

"As the Father loves me, so I also love you. Remain in my love. If you keep my commandments, you will remain in my love, just as I have kept my Father's commandments and remain in his love.

"This is my commandment: love one another as I love you. No one has greater love than this, to lay down one's life for one's friends."

When Jesus had said this, he raised his eyes to heaven and said, "Father, the hour has come. Give glory to your son, so that your son may glorify you.

"I pray not only for them, but also for those who will believe in me through their word, so that they may all be one, as you, Father, are in me and I in you, that they also may be in us, that the world may believe that you sent me. And I have given them the glory you gave me, so that they may be one, as we are one, I in them and you in me, that they may be brought to perfection as one, that the world may know that you sent me, and that you loved them even as you loved me."

## MEDITATION

### The Gift of the Spirit
### Is the Rule of Life for Christian Couples

The new and eternal Covenant not only inspires the couple's life but is fulfilled through it in the sense that the Covenant spreads its own proper energy into the life of the spouses: they love one another not only as Christ loves but also, mysteriously, with the very love of Christ himself. How great is the truth of the vocation to conjugal life according to Christ's words! Let us learn how to be faithful to those words. We find expressed in them the true love of Christ, the love of which he speaks to us in the Gospel: "if anyone loves me, they will keep my word."

Christian spouses, in the dazzling light of heart and spirit, you have discovered how great the sacrament of marriage is! It puts you, so fragile and such sinners, in the presence of God—moreover, in his Trinitarian mystery, as in the mystery of the Incarnate Word! Live in the unity of love that is God's supreme gift!

*SAINT JOHN PAUL II*

## PRAYER

Father, you are infinitely good.
You sanctified marriage

through the great mystery
of Christ's love for the Church,
and you have made it
the sacrament of that covenant of love between Christ
and the Church.

Show us in Christ
the joy of giving oneself totally to the person one loves,
so that we may become one heart, one soul,
and one spirit,
in one sole love.

Through Jesus Christ who was handed over for us,
in the communion of the Holy Spirit.

## ■ THIRD HOUR ■

### *Jesus Accomplishes the Will of the Father*

Word of God          Mark: 14:32-36

THEN THEY CAME to a place named Gethsemane, and he said to his disciples, "Sit here while I pray." He took with him Peter, James, and John, and began to be troubled and distressed. Then he said to them, "My soul is sorrowful even to death. Remain here and keep watch." He advanced a little and fell to the ground and prayed that if it were possible the hour might pass by him; he said, "Abba, Father, all things are possible to you. Take this cup away from me, but not what I will but what you will."

## MEDITATION

### *Christian Spouses Reveal to the Church What Has Come About through the Cross*

Marriage is not "of the world" but "of the Father." The matrimonial covenant is a mystery of unfathomable transcendence; it is a plan that comes from the Creator and is entrusted to fragile human freedom.

Dear spouses, the gap you perceive between the Father's attention and your poor responses must not paralyze you but make you even more dynamic. You have been promised Christ's love; you belong to one another in this love. This love is not only a distant ideal but a present reality when you are united in the Lord, when you pray together, when, like the first time, you move toward one another, when at every moment you say "yes" to his will, when now you invoke him and you ask him, "Be stronger, you in us and between us, stronger than we are by ourselves." Through you, the power of the divine love wills to be made present.

*SAINT JOHN PAUL II*

## PRAYER

Our Father, who art in heaven,
your will be done on earth as it is in heaven—
your will, not ours.

But in your infinite goodness,
it has pleased your holy will to espouse our will,
the will to choose one another in love.

In so consecrating our human love,
you have caught it up into your divine love.
Our love makes manifest the prodigious action
     of your grace.
Our union reveals to the Church and to the world
the marvelous plan of your love.

Stir up in us the will
first to achieve ourselves that union in love
which is your gift to us.
Through Jesus, your beloved Son,
in the communion of the Holy Spirit.

# Adoration
# of the Blessed Sacrament
# in a Time of Need

——————— by Father Sebastian White, o.p. ———————

Adoration of the Blessed Sacrament, whether in a period of public and formal Exposition of the Blessed Sacrament or individually before the tabernacle, even for just a few minutes, is a precious and intimate time of prayer with the Lord. It is a special opportunity for a "heart-to-heart" with the Savior.

Through the eyes of faith, we can see that our sufferings are not an obstacle to the love of Jesus, but the very means by which he draws us close to himself, instructs us in the way of trust and humility, and leads us onward to the place where there will be no more tears or sorrow.

Whether it be a physical illness, a conflict with someone in our life or in our family, the lingering pain and wounds from having been hurt or offended by someone we trusted, sorrow and regret over our own sins or failures, or fear due to uncertainty about the future or how to navigate a difficult situation in our life—whatever the particular form of suffering, that is, whatever trial or need you are facing at this moment, let it be the occasion to draw closer to the Lord. "I whirled out wings.../ And fled with a fling of the heart to the heart of the Host," wrote the poet Gerard Manley Hopkins, s.j., in words that are easily put to memory, and which gently prompt us to do precisely what they say.

The following "hours" may be prayed at your own pace, and need not take an entire hour. You can even pray them at home, certain that God remains present to you, for he encompasses all times and places, and by grace is a stable presence in your soul. See these hours as an inspiration and an invitation to find rest in the Heart of Jesus, and to be completely open before the Lord with whatever burdens might be weighing on your own heart.

～•❖•～

■ FIRST HOUR ■

*Finding Rest*

Word of God                                    Matthew 11:25-30
_____

A T THAT TIME JESUS SAID in reply, "I give praise to you, Father, Lord of heaven and earth, for although you have hidden these things from the wise and the learned you have revealed them to the childlike. Yes, Father, such has been your gracious will. All things have been handed over to me by my Father. No one knows the Son except the Father, and no one knows the Father except the Son and anyone to whom the Son wishes to reveal him.

"Come to me, all you who labor and are burdened, and I will give you rest. Take my yoke upon you and learn from me, for I am meek and humble of heart; and you will find rest for yourselves. For my yoke is easy, and my burden light."

## MEDITATION

### *Come over to me*

Come over to me, all you who are restless,
   and I will teach you how to be quiet,
   how to leave yourself alone.

Come over to me, all you who are anxious,
   even if I don't take your anxiety away,
   I will change it into fresh currency,
   as you turn your cares
   into greater belief in my caring.

Come over to me, all you who are lonely,
   I was lonely too,
   and could find no place
   to lay my head.

Come over to me, all you who worry
   what others really think about you.
   It doesn't matter.
   They misunderstood me, no matter what I did.

Come over to me, all you who are always
   talking and pleading and explaining yourselves
      to others.
   I know you inside out. I know the worst.
   So you can come to me without any explanations.

Come over to me, all you whose great plans
      for yourself have failed.
   You don't know how lucky you are.
   And others too.

Come over to me, all you who can't stand yourselves.
I touched lepers,
and once I called a man out of a tomb
who had been stinking there for four days.
So come over to me—
I can stand just about anything.

Come over to me, all you who can't stand other people.
I know what is behind their misery.
I know the worst in them
as I know it in you.
And I embrace you both.

Come over to me, all you who fret about the past.
I was there, I was part of your past,
and I have forgotten all about it.
So be like me and forget it too.

Come over to me, all you who can't live peacefully
in the present.
Come to me now, without reserve.
That is the way to live peacefully in the present.

Come over to me, all you who fear the future.
Do not fear. I am your future.

*- FATHER THOMAS DOMINIC ROVER, O.P.*

*Father Thomas Dominic Rover († 1997) was a theologian, a playwright, and a poet.*

## PRAYER

Gentle Jesus, Gentle Love: I come to you today confident that you have drawn me here. I know that you only desire my good, and will not permit anything to happen to me that is contrary to your wisdom and your love for me.

I present to you my particular need at this hour [*you can name your intention silently here*].

I trust that you will never abandon me in my sufferings and my trials. Instill within me the wisdom of your sons and daughters, that wisdom that is gained only by depending completely on you. I thank you for remaining among us, and I adore you, Lord Jesus, for you are worthy of all my love. Amen.

■ SECOND HOUR ■

*The Agony of Jesus*

Word of God                                              Luke 22:39-44

T HEN GOING OUT he went, as was his custom, to the Mount of Olives, and the disciples followed him. When he arrived at the place he said to them, "Pray that you may not undergo the test." And withdrawing about a stone's throw from them and kneeling, he prayed, saying, "Father, if you are willing, take this cup away from me; still, not my will but yours be done." [And to strengthen him an angel from heaven appeared to him. He was in such agony and he prayed so fervently that his sweat became like drops of blood falling on the ground.]

## MEDITATION

### *With Christ in the Garden*

I want to assure you of my profound compassion in the painful crisis that you are going through. I understand it thoroughly. But if the waves of suffering and bitterness are violent, do not let yourself go under. Do not let harmful imaginings and debilitating thoughts invade your heart.

Having come to Jesus to share in his sacrifices and his Passion, you have experienced this and continue to go through an agony similar to the one the Savior knew in Gethsemane. Do you know that these anxieties, these dilemmas are not unknown even in the world? It is enough to have received these choice graces and to know at the same time the deep call, the mysterious vocation of suffering.

You cannot relive your life in your mind and imagine that all would have been easier and better in another direction. No, the cross is planted everywhere, in the world. And if the cross plunges more deeply into God's chosen ones, it is because he has himself prepared favorable soil.

A priest said about a woman who was struggling with her feelings: "There are times when you have to take your heart [and] throw it at God's feet...." How hard that is, but how mysterious! At that moment, miracles of grace take place, and one hour of such suffering is equal to a life given over simply to doing the good.

*- SERVANT OF GOD ELISABETH LESEUR*

*Elisabeth Leseur (†1914) was a French married laywoman whose cause for canonization is underway.*

## PRAYER

Lord Jesus, you know what it is like to suffer. Not only did you experience terrible physical pain in being scourged, crowned with thorns, and crucified, but in your agony in the Garden of Gethsemane you endured even the internal agony of facing the cross.

You show us how to respond when we see our own crosses set before us: to unite our wills to the will of God, knowing we can rely on you. I pour out my heart before you today. I offer to you all of my sadness, fears, and anxieties. Fill me with fortitude, confidence, and peace. I unite myself to you, so that my life can be offered up with yours to the heavenly Father.

Amen.

## ■ THIRD HOUR ■

*Trust in God the Father*

Word of God                                      Luke 23:33-35, 39-46

WHEN THEY CAME to the place called the Skull, they crucified him and the criminals there, one on his right, the other on his left. [Then Jesus said, "Father, forgive them, they know not what they do."] They divided his garments by casting lots. The people stood by and watched; the rulers, meanwhile, sneered at him and said, "He saved others, let him save himself if he is the chosen one, the Messiah of God."

Now one of the criminals hanging there reviled Jesus, saying, "Are you not the Messiah? Save yourself and us." The other, however, rebuking him, said in reply, "Have you no fear of God, for you are subject to the same condemnation? And indeed, we have been condemned justly, for the sentence we received corresponds to our crimes, but this man has done nothing criminal." Then he said, "Jesus, remember me when you come into your kingdom." He replied to him, "Amen, I say to you, today you will be with me in Paradise."

It was now about noon and darkness came over the whole land until three in the afternoon because of an eclipse of the sun. Then the veil of the temple was torn down the middle. Jesus cried out in a loud voice, "Father, into your hands I commend my spirit"; and when he had said this he breathed his last.

## MEDITATION

### Ever in God's Hands

Dear brothers and sisters, the words of Jesus on the Cross at the last moments of his earthly life offer us demanding instructions for our prayers, but they also open us to serene trust and firm hope. Jesus, who asks the Father to forgive those who are crucifying him, invites us to take the difficult step of also praying for those who wrong us, who have injured us, ever able to forgive, so that God's light may illuminate their hearts; and he invites us to live in our prayers the same attitude of mercy and love with which God treats us; "forgive us our trespasses and forgive those who trespass against us," we say every day in the Lord's prayer.

At the same time, Jesus, who at the supreme moment of death entrusts himself totally to the hands of God the Father, communicates to us the certainty that, however harsh the trial, however difficult the problems, however acute the suffering may be, we shall never fall from God's hands, those hands that created us, that sustain us and that accompany us on our way through life, because they are guided by an infinite and faithful love.

*- POPE BENEDICT XVI*

*His Holiness Benedict XVI reigned as pope from 2005 until 2013.*

---

## PRAYER

Merciful Jesus, you endured mockery, scorn, and an ignominious death even though you were completely innocent. You bore the insults and revilements silently and patiently, knowing that you were completely secure in the hands of the Father. You were loving to the very end. On the Cross, you not only merited the forgiveness of our own sins, but you also showed us how to forgive those who have sinned against us.

When we suffer unjustly, when we are misunderstood, persecuted, or humiliated, we turn to you for the grace to bear it patiently, for the grace to forgive even our enemies. Lord, we turn to you asking that you give us hearts that love like yours.

Amen.

# Devotion to the Holy Eucharist: Recent Magisterial Statements

## The Eucharist
## and the Holy Sacrifice of the Mass

We believe that the Mass…is the sacrifice of Calvary rendered sacramentally present on our altars. We believe that…the bread and wine consecrated by the priest are changed into the Body and Blood of Christ enthroned gloriously in heaven, and we believe that the mysterious presence of the Lord, under what continues to appear to our senses as before, is a true, real and substantial presence.

Christ cannot be thus present in this sacrament except by the change into his Body of the reality itself of the bread and the change into his Blood of the reality itself of the wine, leaving unchanged only the properties of the bread and wine that our senses perceive. This mysterious change is very appropriately called by the Church transubstantiation. Every theological explanation which seeks some understanding of this mystery must… maintain that in the reality itself, independently of our mind, the bread and wine have ceased to exist after the consecration, so that it is the adorable Body and Blood of the Lord Jesus that from then on are really before us under the sacramental species of bread and wine….

The unique and indivisible existence of the Lord glorious in heaven is not multiplied, but is rendered present by the sacrament in the many places on earth where Mass is celebrated. And this existence remains present, after the sacrifice, in the Blessed Sacrament that is, in the tabernacle, the living heart of each of our churches. And it is our very sweet duty to honor and adore in the blessed host that our eyes see, the Incarnate Word whom they cannot see, and who, without leaving heaven, is made present before us.

*From* Sollemnis Professio Fidei, *an apostolic letter on the Credo of the People of God, proclaimed by Saint Paul VI on June 30, 1968.*

❧◆◆❧

## *The Eucharist and the Love of God*

Since the Eucharistic Mystery was instituted out of love, and makes Christ sacramentally present, it is worthy of thanksgiving and worship. And this worship must be prominent in all our encounters with the Blessed Sacrament, both when we visit our churches and when the sacred species are taken to the sick and administered to them.

Adoration of Christ in this sacrament of love must also find expression in various forms of Eucharistic devotion: personal prayer before the Blessed Sacrament, Hours of Adoration, periods of exposition—short, prolonged and annual (Forty Hours)—Eucharistic benediction, Eucharistic processions, Eucharistic congresses. A particular mention should be made at this point of the Solemnity of the Body and Blood of Christ as an act of public worship rendered to Christ present in the Eucharist, a feast instituted by my predecessor Urban IV in memory of the institution of this great Mystery....

The Church and the world have a great need of Eucharistic worship. Jesus waits for us in this sacrament of love. Let us be generous with our time in going to meet him in adoration and in contemplation that is full of faith and ready to make reparation for the great faults and crimes of the world. May our adoration never cease.

*From* Dominicae Cenae, *an apostolic letter on the Mystery and Worship of the Eucharist, promulgated by Saint John Paul II on February 24, 1980.*

## The Eucharist and the Tabernacle

**1378:** *Worship of the Eucharist.* In the liturgy of the Mass we express our faith in the real presence of Christ under the species of bread and wine by, among other ways, genuflecting or bowing deeply as a sign of adoration of the Lord. "The Catholic Church has always offered and still offers to the sacrament of the Eucharist the cult of adoration, not only during Mass, but also outside of it, reserving the consecrated hosts with the utmost care, exposing them to the solemn veneration of the faithful, and carrying them in procession" (Pope Paul VI, *Mysterium Fidei* 56).

**1379:** The tabernacle was first intended for the reservation of the Eucharist in a worthy place so that it could be brought to the sick and those absent outside of Mass. As faith in the real presence of Christ in his Eucharist deepened, the Church became conscious of the meaning of silent adoration of the Lord present under the Eucharistic species. It is for this reason that the tabernacle should be located in an especially worthy place in the church and should be constructed in such a way that it emphasizes and manifests the truth of the real presence of Christ in the Blessed Sacrament.

**1380:** It is highly fitting that Christ should have wanted to remain present to his Church in this unique way. Since Christ was about to take his departure from his own in his visible form, he wanted to give us his sacramental presence; since he was about to offer himself on the cross to save us, he wanted us to have the memorial of the love with which he loved us to the end (Jn 13:1), even to the giving of his life. In his Eucharistic presence he remains mysteriously in our midst as the one who loved us and gave himself up for us (cf. Gal 2:20), and he remains under signs that express and communicate this love.

*From the* Catechism of the Catholic Church *(1992)*

## *Visiting the Blessed Sacrament*

Adoration of the Blessed Sacrament is a form of Eucharistic [worship] which is particularly widespread in the Church and earnestly recommended to her pastors and faithful. Its initial form derives from Holy Thursday and the altar of repose, following the celebration of the *Coena Domini* Mass. This adoration is a most apt way of expressing the connection between the celebration of the memorial of the Lord's Sacrifice and his continued presence in the Sacrament of the Altar. The reservation of the sacred species, so as to be able to administer Viaticum to the sick at any time, encouraged the practice among the faithful of recollection before the tabernacle and to worship Christ present in the sacrament.

Indeed, this worship of adoration has a sound and firm foundation, especially since faith in the Lord's real presence has as its natural consequence the outward and public manifestation of that belief. Therefore, the devotion prompting the faithful to visit the Blessed Sacrament draws them into an ever deeper share in the paschal mystery and leads them to respond gratefully to the gift of him who through his humanity constantly pours divine life into the members of his Body. Abiding with Christ the Lord, they enjoy his intimate friendship and pour out their hearts before him for themselves and for those dear to them and they pray for the peace and salvation of the world. Offering their entire lives with Christ to the Father in the Holy Spirit, they derive from this sublime colloquy an increase of faith, hope, and charity. Thus they foster those right dispositions that enable them with due devotion to celebrate the memorial of the Lord and receive frequently the bread given us by the Father.

*From the* Directory on Popular Piety and the Liturgy *(2002), by the Congregation for Divine Worship and the Discipline of the Sacraments.*

## *The Eucharist and Prayer*

The *worship of the Eucharist outside of the Mass* is of inestimable value for the life of the Church. This worship is strictly linked to the celebration of the Eucharistic Sacrifice. The presence of Christ under the sacred species reserved after Mass—a presence that lasts as long as the species of bread and of wine remain—derives from the celebration of the sacrifice and is directed towards communion, both sacramental and spiritual….

It is pleasant to spend time with him, to lie close to his breast like the Beloved Disciple (cf. Jn 13:25) and to feel the infinite love present in his heart. If in our time Christians must be distinguished above all by the "art of prayer," how can we not feel a renewed need to spend time in spiritual converse, in silent adoration, in heartfelt love before Christ present in the Most

Holy Sacrament? How often, dear brother and sisters, have I experienced this, and drawn from it strength, consolation, and support!

This practice, repeatedly praised and recommended by the Magisterium, is supported by the example of many saints. Particularly outstanding in this regard was Saint Alphonsus Liguori, who wrote: "Of all devotions, that of adoring Jesus in the Blessed Sacrament is the greatest after the sacraments, the one dearest to God and the one most helpful to us." The Eucharist is a priceless treasure: by not only celebrating it but also by praying before it outside of Mass we are enabled to make contact with the very wellspring of grace.

*From* Ecclesia de Eucharistia, *an encyclical letter on the Eucharist and its relationship to the Church, given by Saint John Paul II on April 17, 2003.*

## *Exposition of the Blessed Sacrament*

Both public and private devotion to the Most Holy Eucharist even outside Mass should be vigorously promoted, for by means of it the faithful give adoration to Christ, truly and really present, the *High Priest of the good things to come* (Heb 9:11) and Redeemer of the whole world. "It is the responsibility of sacred pastors, even by the witness of their life, to support the practice of Eucharistic worship and especially exposition of the Most Holy Sacrament, as well as prayer of adoration before Christ present under the Eucharistic species" (Pope John Paul II, *Ecclesia de Eucharistia*, 25).

The faithful "should not omit making visits during the day to the Most Holy Sacrament, as a proof of gratitude, a pledge of love, and a debt of the adoration due to Christ the Lord who is present in it" (Pope Paul VI, *Mysterium Fidei*, 66). For the contemplation of Jesus present in the Most Holy Sacrament, as a communion of desire, powerfully joins the faithful to Christ, as is splendidly evident in the example of so many saints. "Unless there is a grave reason to the contrary, a church in which the Most Holy Eucharist is reserved should be open to the faithful for at least some hours each day, so that they can spend time in prayer before the Most Holy Sacrament" (Code of Canon Law, 937).

*From* Redemptionis Sacramentum *(2004), an instruction on certain matters to be observed or to be avoided regarding the Most Holy Eucharist, by the Congregation for Divine Worship and the Discipline of the Sacraments.*

## The Eucharist and Adoration

In the Eucharist, the Son of God comes to meet us and desires to become one with us. Eucharistic adoration is simply the natural consequence of the Eucharistic celebration, which is itself the Church's supreme act of adoration. Receiving the Eucharist means adoring him whom we receive. Only in this way do we become one with him, and are given, as it were, a foretaste of the beauty of the heavenly liturgy. The act of adoration outside Mass prolongs and intensifies all that takes place during the liturgical celebration itself. Indeed, "only in adoration can a profound and genuine reception mature. And it is precisely this personal encounter with the Lord that then strengthens the social mission contained in the Eucharist, which seeks to break down not only the walls that separate the Lord and ourselves, but also and especially the walls that separate us from one another" (Address to the Roman Curia, 22 December 2005).

I heartily recommend to the Church's pastors and to the people of God the practice of Eucharistic adoration, both individually and in community. Great benefit would ensue from a suitable catechesis explaining the importance of this act of worship, which enables the faithful to experience the liturgical celebration more fully and more fruitfully. Wherever possible, it would be appropriate, especially in densely populated areas, to set aside specific churches or oratories for perpetual adoration. I also recommend that, in their catechetical training, and especially in their preparation for First Holy Communion, children be taught the meaning and the beauty of spending time with Jesus, and helped to cultivate a sense of awe before his presence in the Eucharist.

*From* Sacramentum Caritatis, *the post-synodal apostolic exhortation on the Sacrament of the Eucharist, given by Pope Benedict XVI on February 22, 2009.*

## *Faith and the Eucharist*

The truth which faith discloses to us is a truth centered on an encounter with Christ, on the contemplation of his life and on the awareness of his presence. Saint Thomas Aquinas speaks of the Apostles' *oculata fides*—a faith which sees!—in the presence of the body of the Risen Lord. With their own eyes they saw the Risen Jesus and they believed; in a word, they were able to peer into the depths of what they were seeing and to confess their faith in the Son of God, seated at the right hand of the Father.

It was only in this way, by taking flesh, by sharing our humanity, that the knowledge proper to love could come to full fruition. For the light of love is born when our hearts are touched and we open ourselves to the interior presence of the beloved, who enables us to recognize his mystery. Thus we can understand why, together with hearing and seeing, Saint John can speak of faith as touch, as he says in his First Letter: *What we have heard, what we have seen with our eyes and touched with our hands, concerning the word of life* (1 Jn 1:1). By his taking flesh and coming among us, Jesus has touched us, and through the sacraments he continues to touch us even today; transforming our hearts, he unceasingly enables us to acknowledge and acclaim him as the Son of God....

The sacramental character of faith finds its highest expression in the Eucharist. The Eucharist is a precious nourishment for faith: an encounter with Christ truly present in the supreme act of his love, the life-giving gift of himself.... In the Eucharist we learn to see the heights and depths of reality. The bread and wine are changed into the Body and Blood of Christ, who becomes present in his passover to the Father: this movement draws us, body and soul, into the movement of all creation towards its fulfillment in God.

*From* Lumen Fidei, *an encyclical published by Pope Francis on June 29, 2013.*

# MEDITATIONS

### *"He is here, in our midst…"*

Lord Jesus, you are here! And you, my brothers, my sisters, my friends. You are here, with me, in his presence!

Lord, two thousand years ago, you willingly mounted the infamous Cross in order then to rise again and to remain forever with us, your brothers and sisters. And you, my brothers, my sisters, my friends. You willingly allow him to embrace you.

We contemplate him. We adore him. We love him. We seek to grow in love for him.

We contemplate him who, in the course of his Passover meal, gave his Body and Blood to his disciples, so as to be with them *always, to the close of the age* (Mt 28:20).

We adore him who is the origin and goal of our faith, him without whom we would not be here, without whom we would not be at all, without whom there would be nothing, absolutely nothing! Him through whom *all things were made* (Jn 1:3), him in whom we were created, for all eternity, him who gave us his own Body and Blood—he is here, in our midst, for us to gaze upon.

We love, and we seek to grow in love for him who is here, in our presence, for us to gaze upon, for us perhaps to question, for us to love.

Whether we are walking or nailed to a bed of suffering; whether we are walking in joy or languishing in the wilderness of the soul: Lord, take us all into your Love; the infinite Love which is eternally the Love of the Father for the Son and the Son for the Father, the Love of the Father and the Son for the Spirit, and the Love of the Spirit for the Father and the Son.

The sacred host exposed to our view speaks of this infinite power of Love manifested on the glorious Cross. The sacred host speaks to us of the incredible abasement of the one who made himself poor so as to make us rich in him, the one who accepted the loss of everything so as to win us for his Father. The sacred host is the living, efficacious and real sacrament of the eternal presence of the Savior of mankind to his Church.

*- POPE BENEDICT XVI*

*His Holiness Benedict XVI reigned as pope from 2005 until 2013.*

## Our Conversation, Our Secret

I adore you, Lord and Creator, hidden in the Blessed Sacrament. I adore you for all the works of your hands that reveal to me so much wisdom, goodness and mercy, O Lord. You have spread so much beauty over the earth and it tells me about your beauty, even though these beautiful things are but a faint reflection of you, incomprehensible beauty. And although you have hidden yourself and concealed your beauty, my eye, enlightened by faith, reaches you and my soul recognizes its Creator, its highest good, and my heart is completely immersed in prayer of adoration.

My Lord and Creator, your goodness encourages me to converse with you. Your mercy abolishes the chasm that separates the Creator from the creature. To converse with you, O Lord, is the delight of my heart. In you I find everything that my heart could desire. Here your light illumines my mind, enabling it to know you more and more deeply. Here streams of graces flow down upon my heart. Here my soul draws eternal life. O my Lord and Creator, you alone, beyond all these gifts, give your own self to me and unite yourself intimately with your miserable creature. Here, without searching for words, our hearts understand each other. Here, no one is able to interrupt our conversation. What I talk to you about, Jesus, is our secret, which creatures shall not know and angels dare not ask about. These are secret acts of forgiveness, known only to Jesus and me; this is the mystery of his mercy, which embraces each soul separately. For this incomprehensible goodness of yours, I adore you, O Lord and Creator, with all my heart and all my soul. And, although my worship is so little and poor, I am at peace because I know that you know it is sincere, however inadequate.

*- SAINT MARIA FAUSTINA KOWALSKA*

*Saint Maria Faustina Kowalska († 1938) was a Polish Sister of Our Lady of Mercy. She was canonized in 2000.*

## *Consumed by the Fire of Love*

How much I love you, O my Jesus. I wish to love you with my whole heart; yet I do not love you enough. My lack of devotion and my sloth make me anxious. I have one desire, that of being near you in the Blessed Sacrament. You are the sweet bridegroom of my soul. My Jesus, my love, my all, gladly would I endure hunger, thirst, heat, and cold to remain always with you in the Blessed Sacrament.

Would that in your Eucharistic presence I might unceasingly weep over my sins. Take entire possession of me. To you I consecrate all the powers of my soul and body, my whole being. Would that I could infuse into all hearts a burning love for you. What great glory would be given to you here on earth, if every heart were an altar on which every human will were laid in perfect conformity with your will to be consumed by the fire of your love.

*- SAINT JOHN NEUMANN*

*Saint John Neumann († 1860) was born in Bohemia. He moved to America, joined the Redemptorists, and was appointed bishop of Philadelphia in 1852.*

## A Life of Sacrifice

You could find no surer bond…to draw me into a more intimate union with your charity than to love the Sacred Heart of our Lord Jesus Christ. I do not doubt that the sacrifice which you want to make of yourself to him so that you may be wholly his, to do and suffer everything for his love, so that you may be able to live completely unto him according to his desires—I do not doubt, I say, that this sacrifice is very pleasing to him. It is a life of sacrifice, of abandonment, and of love. Of sacrifice of all that is most dear to you and of what will cost you the most. Of complete abandonment of yourself to his loving care, taking him as your guide on the way of salvation. You will do nothing unless you ask him for the help of his grace. And this I am sure he will give you to the measure in which you trust him. Moreover, we must live the life of love.

By our humble submission and complete self-effacement it will unite us with him and make us altogether like him in his life of sacrifice, abandonment, and love in the Blessed Sacrament. Love keeps him there as a victim completely and perpetually delivered over to sacrifice for the glory of his Father and for our salvation. Unite yourself with him, then, in all that you do. Refer everything to his glory. Set up your abode in this loving Heart of Jesus and you will there find lasting peace and the strength both to bring to fruition all the good desires he inspires in you, and to avoid every deliberate fault. Place in this Heart all your sufferings and difficulties. Everything that comes from the Sacred Heart is sweet. He changes everything into love.

*– SAINT MARGARET MARY ALACOQUE*

*Saint Margaret Mary Alacoque († 1690) was a Visitandine nun to whom the Lord made many revelations of his Sacred Heart.*

## O Marvelous Sacrament!

Wonderful, indeed, and most worthy of all praise, is the goodness of God, bounteous and unweariedly loving, who, to meet and greet his children, in the sacrament which is the term and final realization of all sacrifices everywhere, dwells without end till the world's end. He gives us for our refreshment the bread of angels, and for our drink strong wine, the blood of his Son, though we are not of his blood. Lowliness, we know, is pleasing to God and it was extolled by Christ; and surely in this sacrament he preaches by the example of an unrivalled lowliness, which disdains no dwelling, but consents to come as a guest to any heart….

O food, truly, of the blessed spirits, you who every day unfailingly does nourish us, and who in yourself does never fail! In the breaking of the bread you are not broken, nor are you divided. You are eaten, but, like the burning bush, you are not consumed. Nay, you continue whole and entire, even as that meal and oil of old which lasted miraculously without diminution or waste (cf. 1 Kings 17:7-16).

O marvelous sacrament in which God lies concealed, and our Jesus, like another Moses, cloaks his face under the creatures he has made! May all generations praise him! Wonderful is this sacrament in which, in virtue of the words of institution, charged with the divine power, the symbolic species are changed into Flesh and Blood; in which…the single and whole Christ exists in different places—as a voice is heard and exists in many places—continuing unchanged, remaining inviolable when partaken, nor suffering any diminution; nay, he is whole and entire and perfect in each and every fragment of the host, as visual appearances are multiplied in a hundred mirrors.

*- SAINT THOMAS AQUINAS*

*Saint Thomas Aquinas († 1274) was a Dominican priest from Italy. He remains one of the Church's premier Doctors. He arranged and composed the liturgical offices for the feast of Corpus Christi.*

## *In the Presence of the Beloved*

Lord Jesus, you are in the Holy Eucharist. You are there, a yard away in the tabernacle. Your body, your soul, your human nature, your divinity, your whole being is there, in its twofold nature. How close you are, my God, my Savior, my Jesus, my brother, my spouse, my beloved.

You were not nearer to the Blessed Virgin during the nine months she carried you in her womb than you are to me when you rest on my tongue at Holy Communion. You were not closer to the Blessed Virgin and Saint Joseph in the caves at Bethlehem or the house at Nazareth or during the flight into Egypt, or at any moment of that divine family life than you are to me at this moment and so many others—in the tabernacle. Saint Mary Magdalene was no closer to you when she sat at your feet at Bethany than I am here at the foot of this altar. You were no nearer to your Apostles when you were sitting in the midst of them than you are to me now, my God. How blessed I am!

It is wonderful, my Lord, to be alone in my cell and converse there with you in the silence of the night—and you are there as God, and by your grace. But to stay in my cell when I could be before the Blessed Sacrament— why, it would be as though Saint Mary Magdalene had left you on your own when you were at Bethany to go and think about you alone in her room! It is a precious and devout thing, O God, to go and kiss the places you made holy during your life on earth—the stones of Gethsemane and Calvary, the ground along the Way of Sorrows, the waves of the Sea of Galilee— but to prefer it to your tabernacle would be to desert the Jesus living beside me, to leave him alone, going away alone to venerate dead stones in places where he is no longer. It would be to leave the room he is in— and with it his divine companionship—to go to kiss the floor of a room he was in, but is in no longer. To leave the tabernacle to go and venerate statues would be to leave the Jesus living at my side to go into another room to greet his portrait.

Is it not true that someone in love feels that he has made perfect use of all the time he spends in the presence of his beloved? Apart from them, is not that time used best which is employed in doing the will or furthering the welfare of his beloved in some other place?

*- BLESSED CHARLES DE FOUCAULD*

*Blessed Charles de Foucauld (✝1916), contemplative and mystic, lived among the Tuareg people of Algeria.*

## *Drawn to Adore*

Adoration becomes seen as precisely the "gravitational pull" of the soul, as that activity which puts a man in his humanity face-to-face with his God. This stance of the creature before his Creator is the one that I think more than ever is needed today by the people of our world who so often have focused their attention on man and have forgotten God who is their goal. It is absolutely necessary that many of us devote ourselves to adoration; we might say it is something needed by the Mystical Body.

At this time when the Holy Spirit is nudging so many people into vocations that involve searching for those who are lost; when so many Christians, driven by the love of Christ, are looking desperately toward those who have gone astray so that they may do everything in their power—save sin—to befriend them wherever they have been led in their estrangement—there is a great need for others to turn to God. Deep inside the human dough there is a need for people who adore, people so convinced of the need for what they are doing that they deprive themselves of all activity on behalf of their human kin. They know that they are answering the essential part of their call by saying again and again to God in the contemporary equivalent of the desert, in the subways, on the highways, in their homes, on their farms: "You are he who is; we are those who are not."

Our time has need of these sacrifices offered amongst people who know nothing of them. There is a need for voices crying in the desert…. "We give you thanks for your great glory, in the total oblation of ourselves."

*- Venerable Madeleine Delbrêl*

*Venerable Madeleine Delbrêl (✝ 1964) was a French laywoman and writer, devoted to caring for the poor and to evangelizing culture.*

## The Grace of Transformation

Jesus gives his Body and his Blood through the bread and wine, to leave us the memorial of his sacrifice of infinite love. And with this "Viaticum" filled with grace, the disciples had everything necessary for their journey through history, to extend to all the Kingdom of God.…

*"The body of Christ is the bond which unites you to him: eat it, or you will have no part in him. The blood is the price he paid for your redemption: drink it, lest you despair of your sinfulness."…*

The Eucharist enables us to abide in him, for it is the bond which unites us to him, it is the fulfillment of the Covenant, the living sign of the love of Christ who humbled and lowered himself in order that we remain united. Participating in the Eucharist and being nourished of him, we are included in a journey which admits no division. Christ present in our midst, in the sign of the bread and wine, demands that the power of love overcome every laceration, and at the same time that it also become communion with the poorest, support for the weak, fraternal attention to those who have difficulty in bearing the weight of daily life....

Jesus poured out his Blood as the price and the laver, so that we might be purified of all sin: not to lose hope, let us look to Him, drink at his font.... Then we will feel the grace of transformation: we will always be poor sinners, but the Blood of Christ will free us from our sins and restore our dignity.

*- POPE FRANCIS*

*His Holiness Pope Francis was elected to the See of Saint Peter in 2013.*

## My Burning Desire

I received a light which revealed to me the infinite lovableness of my God, and at the same time exposed my total inability to love him, to adore him, to bless him, to glorify him, as much as I would have liked and as much as he deserved. In this intense desire that sought to glorify him, I wished that I could increase to infinity the number of angels and saints so that they could praise him with their lips and love him with their hearts. Oh, what pleas I could have poured out to the Holy Spirit in order to obtain my burning desire, begging him to sanctify an immense number of the faithful to whom I could unite myself in order to love and honor my God!

Then, realizing that I had already before me in the Blessed Sacrament more than I was asking for, since the Son of God was sacrificing himself in an infinity of churches, I was greatly consoled that, by uniting myself to Jesus, I had the means of giving to my God all the honor and all the love that he deserved. And not only I, but all creatures have this same power through the same means.

O Lord, how sweet is your Spirit, filling us with blessings, poor servants that we are! That is why you have distributed to us all that you have merited; you give us a share of all you have done for the glory of your Father, so that we may offer it to him as fruit produced by ourselves.

*- FATHER PIERRE CHAUMONOT, S.J.*

*Father Chaumonot († 1693) was a French Jesuit missionary to North America.*

## *Dear Jesus*

Dear Jesus in the Eucharist, I am so very, very happy that you have come into my heart. Never leave my heart, stay forever and ever with me. Jesus I love you so, I want to let myself go in your arms and do what you will with me…. O loving Jesus, give me souls, give me a great many!…

Dear Jesus, today I'm going out, and I'm going to my nuns to tell them I want to make my First Communion at Christmas. Jesus, come soon into my heart, and I'll hug you very tight and kiss you. O Jesus, I want you to stay forever in my heart…. Dear Jesus, I love you so much; I want to tell you again I love you so much.

I give you my heart. Our dear Lady, you are so good, take my heart and carry it to Jesus…. My good Jesus, give me souls, give me a lot of them, I ask you willingly, I ask you so that you make them become good and so that they can come to you in Paradise….

Today I was a bit naughty but you, good Jesus, take your child in your arms…but help me, because without your grace I can do nothing; help me with your grace, help me, for without your grace I can do nothing; I beg you, good Jesus, keep for me always grace of soul….

Dear crucified Jesus, I love you and am so fond of you! I want to be with you on Calvary. Dear Jesus, tell God the Father that I love him, too. Dear Jesus, give me your strength for I need it to bear this pain that I offer for sinners.

Dear Jesus, tell the Holy Spirit to enlighten me with love and to fill me with his seven gifts. Dear Jesus, tell our Lady that I love her and want to be near her. Dear Jesus, I want to tell you again how much I love you.

*- VENERABLE ANTONIETTA MEO*

*Antonietta Meo († 1937), affectionately know as Nennolina, was six and a half years old when she died in Rome, Italy. Her reputation for sanctity spread immediately.*

## Proof of His Love

In order to draw closer to men and give them a more convincing proof of his love, Eternal Wisdom went so far as to become man, even to become a little child, to embrace poverty, and to die upon a cross for them.

How many times while here on earth could he be heard pleading, "Come to me, come to me, all of you.

Do not be afraid, it is I. Why are you afraid? I am just like you; I love you. Are you afraid because you are sinners? But they are the very ones I am looking for; I am the friend of sinners. If it is because you have strayed from the fold through your own fault, then I am the Good Shepherd. If it is because you are weighed down with sin, covered with grime and utterly dejected, then that is just why you should come to me for I will unburden you, purify you, and console you."

Eternal Wisdom, on the one hand, wished to prove his love for man by dying in his place in order to save him, but on the other hand, he could not bear the thought of leaving him. So he devised a marvelous way of dying and living at the same time, and of abiding with man until the end of time. So, in order fully to satisfy his love, he instituted the Sacrament of the Holy Eucharist and went to the extent of changing and overturning nature itself.

He does not conceal himself under a sparkling diamond or some other precious stone, because he does not want to abide with man in an ostentatious manner. But he hides himself under the appearance of a small piece of bread—man's ordinary nourishment—so that when received he might enter the heart of man and there take his delight. *Ardenter amantium hoc est*—Those who love ardently act in this way. "O eternal Wisdom," says a saint, "O God who is truly lavish with himself in his desire to be with man!"

- SAINT LOUIS GRIGNION DE MONTFORT

*Saint Louis de Montfort († 1716) was a great French missionary preacher especially renowned for fostering devotion to the Blessed Virgin Mary.*

❧◇◆◇❧

## Face to Face

It seems to me that nothing better expresses the love in God's heart than the Eucharist: it is union, consummation, he in us, we in him, and isn't that heaven on earth? Heaven in faith while awaiting the face-to-face vision we so desire. Then *we will be satisfied when his glory appears*, when we see him in his light. Don't you find that the thought of this meeting refreshes the soul, this talk with him whom it loves solely? Then everything disappears and it seems that one is already entering into the mystery of God!…

This whole mystery is so much "ours."… I wish to stay always close to him who knows the whole mystery, to hear everything from him…. When we have the Blessed Sacrament exposed in the oratory, those are divine hours spent in this little corner of heaven where we possess the vision in substance under the humble host. Yes, he whom the blessed contemplate in light and we adore in faith is really the same one.

The other day someone wrote me such a beautiful thought; I send it on to you: "Faith is the face-to-face in darkness." Why wouldn't it be so for us, since God is in us and since he asks only to take possession of us as he took possession of the saints? Only, they were always attentive, as Père Vallée says: "They are silent, recollected, and their only activity is to be the being who receives."… Let us make a dwelling for him in our soul that is wholly at peace…. And may our life be a continual communion, a wholly simple movement toward God.

*- SAINT ELIZABETH OF THE TRINITY*

*Saint Elizabeth of the Trinity († 1906) was a French Carmelite nun and mystical writer.*

## *Love for Eternal Wisdom*

A seasoned friend of God should always have some good model or saying in the mouth of his soul to chew on that will inflame his heart for God, because therein lies the most sublime thing we can attain on earth—that we often reflect on our divine Beloved, that we often send out our hearts to him, often speak of him, take in his words of love, for his sake abandon or perform all things, and have no one but him alone as the focus of our attention.

Our eye should look upon him with love. Our ear should open to his bidding. Our heart, mind, and spirit should lovingly embrace him. If we make him angry, we should beg his pardon. If he tries us, we should endure him. When he hides, we should seek our dear love and never give up until we find him again and again. When we find him, we should hold him tenderly and reverently. Whether we are at rest or going somewhere, whether we are eating or drinking, the golden clasp IHS should be inscribed on our heart. When we can do nothing else, we should press him with our eyes into our soul. We should turn over his tender name in our mouth. We should be so intent on this while awake that we dream about it at night. Let us say with the prophet, *O dear God, eternal Wisdom, how good you are to the soul that seeks you, that longs for you alone.*

Realize that this is the best habit you can have, for constant prayer is the crown of all activity. Everything else should be directed to it as to its goal. What other activity is there in heaven but gazing at and loving the object of all love, loving it and praising it? Therefore, the more dearly we press the divine object of our love into our hearts, and the more often we look upon him and intimately embrace him with the arms of our hearts, the more lovingly shall we be embraced by him here and in our eternal happiness.

*- BLESSED HENRY SUSO*

*Blessed Henry Suso († 1366) was a German Dominican priest whose mystical writings focus on divine wisdom and love for Christ's Passion.*

## *Love of Loves*

Our most loving Savior, knowing that his hour was now come for leaving this earth, desired, before he went to die for us, to leave us the greatest possible mark of his love; and this was the gift of the most holy sacrament.

Saint Bernardine of Siena remarks that men remember more continually and love more tenderly the signs of love that are shown to them in the hour of death. Hence it is the custom that friends, when about to die, leave to those persons whom they have loved some gift, such as a garment or a ring, as a memorial of their affection. But what have you, O my Jesus, left us, when quitting this world in memory of your love? Not, indeed, a garment or a ring, but your own body, your blood, your soul, your divinity, your whole self, without reserve. "He gave you all," says Saint John Chrysostom, "[and] he left nothing for himself." Saint Bernardine of Siena says that Jesus Christ, burning with love for us, and not content with being prepared to give his life for us, was constrained by the excess of his love to work a greater work before he died; and this was to give his own body for our food.

This sacrament, therefore, was rightly named by Saint Thomas "the sacrament of love, the pledge of love...." Saint Bernard calls this sacrament "the love of loves"; because this gift comprehends all the other gifts bestowed upon us by our Lord.... The Eucharist is not only a pledge of the love of Jesus Christ, but of paradise, which he desires also to give us. "In which," says the Church, "a pledge of future glory is given us." Hence Saint Philip Neri could find no other name for Jesus Christ in the sacrament save that of "love"; and so, when the holy Viaticum was brought to him, he was heard to exclaim, "Behold my love; give me my love."

*- SAINT ALPHONSUS LIGUORI*

*Saint Alphonsus Liguori († 1787), a bishop, founded the Redemptorists. He is a Doctor of the Church.*

## *Listening to Jesus*

Jesus says: "I love you because I gave my life for you. I love you because you listen to me, you begin to listen to me; you will listen to me more and more. I love you because you cannot do without me.... God alone is. I am your life. Do you understand that? I am as inseparable from you as your breathing, as the breath within your soul. I am so near to you. It is I who incline you to be patient, to be gentle, to accept things....

"Ask all of me; ask every day, every morning what is necessary for the day, for yourself and for the human race. Ask ceaselessly, without wearying. It is my joy to answer! I always answer; but my answer is varied. You would understand it better if you knew how to live by faith. Do not be disturbed at repeating to your Father what I say to you; there is nothing extraordinary in it. I speak to each soul; if there are some who do not hear me, it is because they do not listen to me. There must be a profound silence, because my voice is soft. The soul must be freed from all engrossing thoughts; I must be loved in spirit and in truth—the whole being must be in the truth.

"Respond more quickly to my voice, I who await you, I who have loved you for so long. Leave all. Let there no longer be anything else in the world for you but the love between you and me. Give, simplify your life, free yourself. Be altogether poor so as to be altogether mine. Be more simple with your Father; show yourself as you are…. He should be able to read your heart without any effort, like an open book. Do not be uneasy: ask his advice about everything that makes you anxious, and do exactly what he tells you."

*- SISTER MARY OF THE HOLY TRINITY*

*Sister Mary of the Holy Trinity († 1942) was a Poor Clare of Jerusalem.*

## *Devotion to the Sacred Heart*

The Heart of Jesus glowed with that divine and uninterrupted fire to the last instant of its mortal life, and will ever thus burn for all eternity. By one single act of the love of God produced by it, the divine majesty is infinitely more honored than it could possibly be by the united love of all creatures even possible during a whole eternity. How noble then must that Heart be, the function whereof is to receive continually the impressions of this sacred love, and produce the highest acts thereof uninterruptedly for all eternity....

It is plain from all this, that we do not mean to honor the Sacred Heart of Jesus barely as an inanimate and lifeless Heart, but we consider it as united to the divine person and as the chief instrument of the most holy soul that ever was....

We are to consider the Sacred Heart of Jesus under two different aspects; on one side, as a Heart full of love, and breathing nothing but the salvation of mankind; on the other side, as a Heart that is offended, insulted and despised by unthinking man, by sinners void of all sense of gratitude and unaffected by his love. The inclination of this adorable Heart to reconcile man to God, and earth to heaven, must raise in us sentiments of the most ardent love and feelings of the greatest sorrow, to dispose us for a reparation of the wrongs and outrages it daily suffers.

The end therefore proposed by this devotion, to which the faithful are earnestly invited, is in the first place to honor by frequent acts of love and adoration, and by all manner of submission and homage the unbounded love of Jesus for us throughout the whole course of his mortal life, but chiefly in the Sacrament of the Holy Eucharist, the sum and abridgement of all his wonders, where he still burns with the love of us. In the next place it is to share in his grief and to make amends on our part for those many insults his love for us exposed him to during his mortal life, and still now exposes him to every day in the Blessed Sacrament.

*- THE PIOUS GUIDE TO PRAYER AND DEVOTION*

*The Pious Guide to Prayer and Devotion (1792) was one of the first English-language books written by American Jesuits and published in the United States for use by the Catholic laity.*

## Bonds of Sublime Love

**W**hat tenderness there is in Jesus' love for man! In his infinite goodness, he established, with each of us, bonds of sublime love! He comes to dwell in our hearts with his Body, Soul, and Divinity. What a marvelous gift! Jesus' love has no limits. With him, we form one single body.

Jesus could have limited his presence only to the celebration of Mass, but no! He wanted to make a permanent dwelling among us. Night and day he awaits us and offers himself to us at all times. Like a most tender mother, he opens his arms to us. He is there generously to give us his gifts. He is there to draw us to him and lead us to paradise with him. Oh! Let us go visit him often.

*- Saint John Bosco*

*Saint John Bosco († 1888) founded the Salesians of Don Bosco.*

---

## Inexhaustible Love

**O**ur Lord sends neither angels nor ministers to assure us of his love; he comes in person. Love will have no go-between. And so he perpetuates himself only to tell us over and over again: "I love you. You see that I love you!"

Our Lord was so afraid we might forget him that he took up his abode among us. He made his home with us so that we might not be able to think of him without thinking of his love. By giving himself thus and insisting on this gift, he hoped not to be forgotten.

Whoever gives serious thought to the Eucharist, and especially whoever partakes of it, cannot help feeling that our Lord loves him. He feels that in him he has a father. He feels that he is loved as a child and that he has a right to come to his Father and speak to him. In church, at the foot of the tabernacle, he is in his Father's home.

Does our Lord not give himself whole and entire to each one? And if a greater number come to receive him, does he divide himself up? Does he give less to each one? If the church is full of adorers, can they not all pray to Jesus and converse with him? Is not each one listened to and his prayer granted as if he were the only one in church?

Such is the personal love of Jesus for us. Each one may take it all for himself and wrong no one; the sun gives all its light to each and every one of us; the ocean belongs whole and entire to each and every fish. Jesus is greater than us all. He is inexhaustible.

*- SAINT PETER JULIAN EYMARD*

*Saint Peter Julian Eymard († 1868) founded the Congregation of the Blessed Sacrament.*

## Contemplating the Sacred Mysteries

If the soul wants and desires to understand and to say something about God, ordainer, sovereign, uncreated, and incarnate; and it wishes to know something about matters concerning him; and especially if it wants to know something concerning this most high and holy sacrament which God, as ordainer, ordains to be celebrated daily through the words of his priest, his minister, then such a soul ought to be transformed totally in God through love. Once transformed into him, the soul should place itself in his presence, stay there, and enter within God himself and not remain outside him. The following is what I mean by "being in the presence of God" and "entering within him": to consider and perceive him, who is the ordainer and highest uncreated good.

Let the soul consider, first of all, who and what God is in himself. Then, elevated out of itself into God, it can see him who is invisible, know him who is unknowable, feel him who is imperceptible, comprehend him who is incomprehensible. And this is so because the soul sees, knows, feels, and comprehends God as invisible light, incomprehensible, and unknown good. Comprehending, seeing, knowing, and feeling God, the soul, according to its capacity, expands in him and becomes filled with him through love. It finds its delight in God and God finds his delight in it and with it. The soul, then, experiences and possesses God's sweetness more from what it does not comprehend than from what it comprehends, more from what it does not see than from what it sees, more from what it does not feel than from what it feels, more, finally, from what it does not know than from what it knows.

It seems to me that this is the reason that no matter how perfect the soul, even if it is as perfect as that of the Blessed Virgin, it comprehends nothing of God, the ordainer, uncreated, and infinite. From looking at what it sees, feels, and knows, it sees, feels, and knows that it cannot see, feel, and know. Therefore, concerning, and in, this mystery and most high sacrament the soul must ponder over, see, feel, and know its uncreated ordainer, and who he is.

It should also see and consider what it is concerning him and in him that creates order, that is, what he did and does to be ordainer of this mystery. I do not know what name to give it unless it be "love without measure," for he is the ordainer, the good God, infinite love.

*- SAINT ANGELA OF FOLIGNO*

*Saint Angela of Foligno († 1309) was a wife and mother who later became a Franciscan tertiary and an esteemed mystical writer.*

---

## *Our Brother, Our Food*

We ought to pay God honor in every way we can think of; for every creature, even the tiny insects, if they could only understand, would be bound to look up at the Blessed Sacrament and bow down before him. Yet there is a higher level at which we can praise God. We can love him ardently, and want him in the depths of our souls, with all our intellect and all our reason. This is far better than any outward act that we can perform. Still, there is another level, even higher: to acknowledge in the depths of our souls that God is so great and we are so small that it is impossible for us to praise him. This is in itself an act of praise far beyond all words and thoughts and understanding.

A great teacher has said: "The man who speaks best about God is the man who has recognized his inward riches and is silent."… God's incomprehensible glory is so great that merely to acknowledge it comprehends all words and all forms. The soul praises him by being engulfed in him, losing itself in him, sinking down and melting into him, sharing in God's own praising and thanking of himself for his own being.

Our dear Lord said: *My flesh is truly food, and my blood is truly drink; whoever feeds on me remains in me, and I in him.* It was not enough for him to become our brother, to take upon himself…human nature. It was not enough that he should become man so that man might become God. He even wanted to be our food as well. Saint Augustine said: "There is no people so great as the Christian people; none of them has a god so close to them as our God is to us." We feed upon our God. How wonderful and inexpressible is this love of his, which found this marvelous way for him to come to us! His love is beyond all comprehension, and it should pierce us all to the heart that he shows such incomparable love toward us.

*- FATHER JOHN TAULER, O.P.*

*Father Tauler (†1361) was a German Dominican priest, a popular preacher, and a mystical theologian.*

## The Silence of Eternity

Contemplative silence can frighten us. It is like a big wave that carries us, without being able to drown us, and causes us to end up on fearsome shores. For man then finds himself facing the terrifying immensity of the mystery. I do not think it is possible to approach God's majesty without trembling in dread and astonishment. Our ancestors were often physically moved by a great fear that simultaneously expressed admiration, respect, and a religious fear of the blazing furnace of God's transcendence.

God's silence is a consuming fire for the man who approaches him. Through this divine silence, man becomes a bit estranged from this world. He is separated from the earth and from himself. Silence impels us toward an unknown land that is God. And this land becomes our true homeland. Through silence, we return to our heavenly origin, where there is nothing but calm, peace, repose, silent contemplation, and adoration of the radiant face of God.

All the great saints were familiar with this incomparable experience. When their prayers led them to the threshold of the Eternal One's silence, they sensed how close and immense God became. They remained wordlessly in the presence of the Father. The more they ascended toward God, the more silent they became. Saint Philip Neri and Saint Thérèse of Lisieux were confronted with a reality they could not comprehend, but they saw with their own eyes the Infinite and the splendor of love. This immensity came to draw them into a grand silence of adoration and interior peace.

Contemplative silence is silence with God. This silence is clinging to God, appearing before God, and placing oneself in his presence, offering oneself to him, mortifying oneself in him, adoring, loving, and hearing him, listening to him and resting in him. This is the silence of eternity, the union of the soul with God.

*- CARDINAL ROBERT SARAH*

*Cardinal Sarah is the Prefect of the Congregation for Divine Worship and the Discipline of the Sacraments.*

## The Eucharistic Heart of Jesus

*Jesus knowing that his hour was come, that he should pass out of this world to the Father: having loved his own who were in the world, he loved them unto the end* (Jn 13:1). A father who is about to die wishes to leave to his children a supreme proof of his love for them. Often such a father cannot find words to express his love and he remains silent with a silence that is more eloquent than speech. When Jesus was about to die he found not only the words to express his meaning but also the words that would make his meaning a reality, the words of transubstantiation. He gave us the Eucharist as a testament, and in this sacrament he left to us his own divine Person….

True and generous love, by which we wish others well and do them good, leads us to bend down toward them if they are below us. It inspires us to unite ourselves to them in perfect union of thought, desire, and will, to devote ourselves to them, to sacrifice ourselves if necessary to make them better, and to encourage them to reach out beyond themselves and attain their destiny.

When our Lord was about to deprive us of his sensible presence, he wished to leave himself to us in person under the Eucharistic veils. Loving us as he did, he could not bend down any lower toward us, toward the lowliest, the poorest…. There was no way by which he could unite himself or give himself more completely to each of us.

There are times when we yearn for the real presence of loved ones who are no more. The Eucharistic Heart of the Savior has given us the real presence of his Body, his Blood, his Soul, and his Divinity. Everywhere on earth wherever there is a consecrated host in a tabernacle, even in the most far-flung missions, he remains with us, the sweet companion of our exile. He is in each tabernacle, patiently waiting for us, eager to grant us favors, yearning for our prayers....

The practical consequence of this truth is that the Eucharistic Heart of Jesus is by no means the object of an affected devotion. It is the supreme model of the perfect gift of self, a gift that in our own lives should become more generous with each passing day.... As a stone gathers momentum in its fall toward the earth that attracts it, so should souls tend toward God with increasing speed as they come closer to him and are powerfully attracted to him. The Eucharistic Heart of Jesus yearns to attract our souls to itself.

*- FATHER REGINALD GARRIGOU-LAGRANGE, O.P.*

*Father Garrigou-Lagrange († 1964) was a Dominican theologian who produced numerous books and articles. He was the theology doctoral advisor of the future Saint John Paul II.*

### Seeing, Believing, Listening, Loving

Long ago and far away, an ordinary man called John laid his head on the breast of Christ and listened to the heartbeats of the Lord. Who can venture to guess what that man felt as he heard the beat of that mighty heart? None of us can ever be in his place, but all of us could hear—if we would but listen—the heartbeats of God, the song of love that he sings to us, whom he has loved so much.

If we meditated on the Most Holy Sacrament of the Eucharist, we would not only hear his heartbeats, we would hear our own hearts beating in unison with his. We would be united with our Lord and our God. God's heart is the only true resting place for all of us, the real oasis to which God calls us. But the key to his heart is identification with him and with all those he calls his little ones.

This deep love of humanity requires an enlargement of heart that is so great that we could not aspire to it unless God showed us the way. We must pray for that enlargement of heart.

*- SERVANT OF GOD CATHERINE DE HUECK DOHERTY*

*Catherine de Hueck Doherty (✝ 1985) was born in Russia and was the foundress of Madonna House in Combermere, Canada.*

## Hidden Grandeur

When I approached to receive Communion and recalled the extraordinary majesty I had seen and considered that it was present in the Blessed Sacrament (the Lord often desires that I behold it in the host), my hair stood on end; the whole experience seemed to annihilate me. O my Lord! If you did not hide your grandeur, who would approach so often a union of something so dirty and miserable with such great majesty! May the angels and all creatures praise you, for you so measure things in accordance with our weakness that when we rejoice in your sovereign favors your great power does not so frighten us that, weak and wretched people, we would not dare enjoy them....

O wealth of the poor, how admirably you know how to sustain souls! And without their seeing such great wealth, you show it to them little by little. When I behold majesty as extraordinary as this concealed in something as small as the Host, it happens afterward that I marvel at wisdom so wonderful, and I fail to know how the Lord gives me the courage or strength to approach him. If he who has granted, and still does grant me so many favors, did not give this strength, it would be impossible to conceal the fact or resist shouting aloud about marvels so great. For what will a wretched person, like myself, who is weighted down with abominations and who has wasted his life with so little fear of God, feel when he sees he is approaching this Lord of such powerful majesty and that his Lord desires that the soul behold it? How will a mouth that has spoken so many words against this very Lord be united with that most glorious body, which abounds in purity and compassion? For the love that face shows, so beautiful in tenderness and affability, makes the soul much more sorrowful and afflicted for not having served him than does the majesty it beholds in him cause it to fear. But how could I have experienced twice what I saw and am about to describe?

*- SAINT TERESA OF ÁVILA*

*Saint Teresa of Ávila († 1582), Doctor of the Church, reformed the Carmelite Order.*

## Immortal Food

As soon as I called to mind the beauty of undefiled love, its light suddenly appeared in my heart. I have been ravished with its delight and have ceased to perceive outward things; I have lost all sense of this life and have forgotten the things that are at hand. Yet again—I am at a loss how to say it—it has removed far from me and left me to lament my own weakness.

O all-desirable love, how happy is he who has embraced you, for he will no longer have a passionate desire to embrace any earthly beauty! Happy is he who is moved by divine love to cling to you! He will deny the whole world, yet as he associates with all men he will be wholly untainted. Happy is he who caresses your beauty and with infinite desire delights therein, for he will be spiritually sanctified by the water and blood (cf. Jn. 19:34) that in all purity issue from you! Happy is he who passionately embraces you, for he will be wondrously changed! In spirit and in soul he will rejoice, because you are the ineffable joy. Happy is he who gains possession of you, for he will count the treasures of the world as nothing, for you are indeed the truly inexhaustible riches. Happy and triply happy is he whom you accept, for though he be without any visible glory he will be more glorious than all that is glorious, more honored and august than all that is honored.

Worthy of praise is he who pursues you; even more praiseworthy is he who has found you; more blessed he who is loved by you, received by you, taught by you, he who dwells in you and is fed by you with Christ, the immortal food, Christ our God!

*- SAINT SYMEON THE NEW THEOLOGIAN*

*Saint Symeon († 1022) was a spiritual master and a monk in Constantinople.*

❧◇◆◇❧

## Paradise in the Holy Eucharist

As for the dangers of the soul, to speak frankly, there are none for him who brings the fear and love of God with him to the country of the Hurons. On the contrary, I find unparalleled opportunities for acquiring perfection. Is it not a great deal to have no other attraction in your food, clothing, and sleep than that of satisfying your simplest needs? Is it not a glorious opportunity to unite your soul with God there where no creature whatsoever gives you reason to spend your affection upon it, and when your exercises of devotion lead you gently to interior contemplation?…

It is true that we do not have here the exterior solemnity of worship that awakens and sustains devotion. The only external sign of our holy religion that we have is the Blessed Sacrament of the Altar. To its marvels we must open the eyes of our faith without the aid of any sensible mark of its grandeur, like the Magi of old in the stable. It seems, moreover, that God supplies what we lack and rewards us with grace for having transported the holy sacrament beyond so many seas and having found an abode for it in these poor cabins…. These good people hardly ever see either *Church* or altar, but the little they do see is doubly worth what they would be able to perceive in full liberty.

Can you imagine the consolation there is in prostrating yourself once in a while before a cross that has been erected in the midst of this barbarism? Can you conceive the comfort you receive in the midst of even the most trifling domestic occupations when you turn your eyes toward the tabernacle, or enter the room that the Son of God has been pleased to take for his own in our tiny dwelling? Is this not living in paradise day and night, being separated from this well-beloved of nations only by a piece of bark or a branch of a tree?

*- Saint John de Brébeuf*

*Saint John de Brébeuf († 1649) was a French Jesuit priest and is one of the proto-martyrs of North America.*

## *He Is My Heaven*

O Jesus, grant me I beg you
The bread of strength to break my will and to weld it to yours.
The bread of interior mortification,
The bread of detachment from creatures.
The bread of patience to bear the pains which my heart suffers.
O Jesus, you wish me crucified, *fiat*.
O Mary, Mother of Sorrows, at the foot of the Cross you received the title of our Mother. I am the child of your sorrows, the child of Calvary. Mary, my tender Mother, here is your child, who can do no more. Have pity on me. Grant that I may be in heaven one day with you. You who have seen and felt the terrible desolation of your dear Son, assist me now in mine.

Nothing means anything any more to me but Jesus. Neither places nor things nor persons nor ideas nor feelings nor honors nor sufferings can turn me away from Jesus. For me he is all honor and charm and heart and spirit. Him whom I love is my native land, he is my heaven already! My treasure! My love! My happiness consists only in Jesus and in him crucified…in an intimate union with Jesus, heart to heart with Jesus like Saint John, in purity and love.

*- SAINT BERNADETTE SOUBIROUS*

*Saint Bernadette Soubirous († 1879) was favored with a series of visions of the Blessed Virgin Mary at Lourdes. Her body remains incorrupt.*

## *Food of the Soul*

When God desired to give a food to our soul to sustain it in the pilgrimage of life, he looked upon creation and found nothing that was worthy of it. Then he turned again to himself, and resolved to give himself…. O my soul, how great you are, since only God can satisfy you! The food of the soul is the body and blood of a God. O glorious food! The soul can feed only on God; only God can suffice it; only God can fill it; only God can satiate its hunger. Its God is absolutely necessary to it….

My God, how can it be that Christians actually remain so long without giving this food to their poor souls? They leave them to die of want. They are close to this glorious sacrament, like a person dying of thirst by the side of a river, when he has only to bend his head… like a person remaining in poverty with a treasury close beside him, when he has only to stretch out his hand. My God, what misery and blindness…when they have so many remedies for healing their souls, and such food for preserving their health!…

Do not say, to justify your estrangement from the holy table, that you have too much to do. Has not the divine Savior said: *Come to me all you that labor and are exhausted: come to me, I will relieve you.* Can you resist an invitation so full of love and tenderness? Do not say that you are not worthy of it. It is true you are not worthy, but you have need of it. If our Lord had been thinking of our worthiness he would never have instituted his glorious sacrament of love, for no one in the world is worthy of it—not the saints, nor the angels, nor archangels, nor the Blessed Virgin…but he was thinking of our needs.

Do not say that you are sinners, that you are too wretched, and that that is why you dare not approach it. You might just as well say that you are too ill, and that that is why you will not try any remedy nor send for the doctor.

*- Saint John Vianney*

*Saint John Vianney, the Curé of Ars (†1859), is the patron of priests.*

---

## The Door of Salvation

*T*he thoughts of his Heart—the Heart of Jesus—*are to all generations: to deliver them from death, to feed them in time of famine.* The Heart of Jesus is always in search of souls to save, to free from the snares of sin, to wash in his Blood, to feed with his Body. The Heart of Jesus is always living in the Eucharist to satisfy the hunger of all who long for him, to welcome and console all those who, disillusioned by the vicissitudes of life, take refuge in him, seeking peace and refreshment. Jesus himself is our support on the hard road of life. *Take up my yoke upon you and learn of me, because*

*I am meek and humble of heart, and you shall find rest for your souls, alleluia.* It is impossible to eliminate sorrow from our life; yet if we live for Jesus we can suffer in peace and find in the Heart of Jesus repose for our weary soul....

Jesus presents himself as the door that leads to salvation. *I am the door. By me if any man enters in he shall be saved* (Jn 10:9). This door is his Heart, which, wounded for us, has brought us into life. By love alone can we penetrate this mystery of infinite love, but not any kind of love will suffice. As Saint Paul says, we must *be rooted and founded in charity*. Only thus shall we be able *to know...the charity of Christ which surpasses all knowledge, that [we] may be filled unto all the fullness of God* (Eph 3:17, 19).

*- Father Gabriel of Saint Mary Magdalen, o.c.d.*

*Father Gabriel of Saint Mary Magdalen († 1952) was a Belgian Carmelite priest, teacher, and spiritual director.*

## Bread of Life

When, in prayer, we ask Our Lord to tell us why he willed, in his eternal Wisdom, to establish this ineffable sacrament, what does he reply?

To begin with, he repeats those same words with which he first announced the institution of the Eucharist to the Jews. *As the Living Father hath sent me and I live by the Father, so he that eateth me, the same also shall live by me.* It is as if he said: my desire is to communicate my divine life to you. I hold my being, my life, all, from my Father, and because I hold all from him, I live only for him; I desire with an intense desire that you, likewise, holding all from me, live only for me. Your corporal life is sustained and developed by food; I will to be the food of your soul, so as to preserve and develop its life which is myself. He that eats me, lives by my life; I possess the fullness of grace, and those to whom I give myself as food partake of this grace. The Father has life in himself, but he has given to the Son also to have life in himself. And because I possess this life I am come to give it fully and abundantly. I give you life because I give myself as food. I am the Living Bread, the Bread of Life come down from heaven so as to give you eternal life; that Bread which gives the heavenly life, the everlasting life, of which grace is the dawn. The Jews in the desert did eat manna, a corruptible food; but I am the ever Living Bread, ever needful for your souls, for *except you eat the flesh of the Son of Man, and drink his blood, you shall not have life in you.*

Such are the very words of Jesus. It is therefore not only in order that we may adore him, and offer him to his Father as infinite satisfaction, that Christ renders himself present on the altar; it is not only to visit us that he comes, but it is that we may eat him as the food of our souls, and that eating him, we may have life, the life of grace here below, the life of glory hereafter.

*- Blessed Columba Marmion*

*Blessed Columba († 1923) was abbot of the Benedictine abbey of Maredsous, Belgium.*

≈◇◇≈

## Drawn to Him

It is estimated that in every second of the day and night four elevations of the Host take place.

I never cease to wonder at this, or to rejoice in the knowledge that there is never a second of one's life in which one cannot lift up one's heart to God in the heart of Christ lifted up in the Host. I think, too, of all the places in the world where the Mass is being celebrated; of how Christ, who began his earthly life in a stable and ended it on a scaffold, has penetrated into every place and circumstance of human life, and has gathered every fragment of man's love to be offered in sacrifice.

Think of all the places where Mass is being celebrated at this present moment, the very moment in which you are reading this page; all the cathedrals and all the churches of the world, all the tin huts and mud huts and make-shifts that are the best man can do in many mission fields…. In ships out on the deep seas, on battlefields and camps, in prisons and hospital wards, in the desert and the jungle, in the great cities of the world, in the cottages of faithful peasants in persecuted countries, and under the tall trees of lonely forests of exile.

Think too how everywhere where Christ is lifted up men are bowed down in adoration, soldiers, sailors, airmen, fishermen, men of every country, of every color, rich men and poor men, free men and prisoners, old men and young men, men of every craft and trade and profession, all adoring God, all in communion with one another, all in communion with the Holy Father, all in communion with you and me. *And I, if I be lifted up, will draw all men to me.*

*- CARYLL HOUSELANDER*

*Caryll Houselander († 1954) was a British author, poet, and spiritual teacher.*

## *Trusting in Mercy*

Lord Jesus Christ
by the Father's plan and by the working
of the Holy Spirit
of your own free will you died
and mercifully redeemed the world
from sin and everlasting death.
I adore and venerate you
as much as ever I can,
though my love is so cold, my devotion so poor.
Thank you for the good gift
of this your holy Body and Blood,
which I desire to receive, as cleansing from sin,
and for a defense against it.

Lord, I acknowledge that I am far from worthy
to approach and touch this sacrament;
but I trust in that mercy
which caused you to lay down your life for sinners
that they might be justified,
and because you gave yourself
willingly as a holy sacrifice to the Father.
A sinner, I presume to receive these gifts
so that I may be justified by them.
I beg and pray you, therefore, merciful lover of men,

let not that which you have given
for the cleansing of sins
be unto me the increase of sin,
but rather for forgiveness and protection.

Make me, O Lord, so to perceive with lips and heart
and know by faith and by love,
that by virtue of this sacrament I may deserve to be
planted in the likeness of your Death and Resurrection,
by mortifying the old man,
and by renewal of the life of righteousness.
May I be worthy to be incorporated into your body
"which is the Church,"
so that I may be your member
and you may be my Head,
and that I may remain in you and you in me.
Then at the resurrection you will refashion
the body of my humiliation
according to the body of your glory,
as you promised by your Apostle,
and I shall rejoice in you forever
to your glory,
who with the Father and the Holy Spirit
lives and reigns forever. Amen.

*- SAINT ANSELM*

*Saint Anselm († 1109) was an abbot, bishop, philosopher, and theologian.*

## O Sacred Host!

**C**an the soul explain what a consecrated host is,
what it feels on seeing Jesus in this hidden manner,

and when approaching him in the host, and what is the sensation produced by divine contact with him in Holy Communion?

Who can see you, O sacred host, without being moved? Who is not attracted by your divine beauty? Who on feeling your burning rays does not feel your warmth, and drink of the fountain of life?

Who does not feel his faith, his hope, and his love increase in the presence of your incomprehensible abasement?

Who can contemplate you and not repent of his sins? I believe that if there were no consecrated hosts in the world, I would have no difficulty in sacrificing the sight of my eyes. For the only real, ardent, and profound desire I have is to see you, you alone, my Jesus! I place all my happiness in looking at you! Three times as happy as now would be he who could pass his life in doing nothing else but looking at you!

O sacred host, I carry your image engraved in my memory, but far more in my heart. I always seek you in the ciborium, in the tabernacle, in the monstrance, as my eyes and my thoughts pierce brick walls, silk, precious metals, and even the appearance of bread that hides you, my Jesus.

*- BLESSED CONCEPCIÓN CABRERA DE ARMIDA*

*Blessed Concepción, "Conchita" († 1937), was a wife, mother, and widow in Mexico. She was the first Mexican laywoman to be beatified.*

## The Power of Faith

**W**e must, then, have faith and not be dispirited. We must not be stopped by any kind of human calculation.

To overcome the obstacles we have to throw ourselves into the task so that the very effort we make will open up new paths. Personal holiness, giving oneself to God, is the one cure that overcomes any difficulty.

Being holy means living exactly as our Father in heaven wants us to live. You will say that it is difficult. It is. The ideal is a very high one. And yet it is also easy. It is within our reach. When a person becomes ill there may be no appropriate medicine. But in supernatural affairs, it is not like that. The medicine is always at hand. It is Jesus Christ, present, in the Holy Eucharist, and he also gives us his grace in the other sacraments that he established.

Let us say again, in word and in action: "Lord, I trust in you; your ordinary providence, your help each day, is all I need." We do not have to ask God to perform great miracles. Rather, we have to beg him to increase our faith, to enlighten our intellect, and strengthen our will. Jesus always stays by our side and is always himself.

*- SAINT JOSEMARÍA ESCRIVÁ*

*Saint Josemaría Escrivá († 1975) was the founder of Opus Dei.*

## To Gaze upon the Sun of Love

O my Jesus! I love you! I love the Church, my Mother! I recall that "the smallest act of pure love is of more value to her than all other works together" (Saint John of the Cross). But is pure love in my heart? Are my measureless desires only but a dream, a folly? Ah! if this be so, Jesus, then enlighten me, for you know I am seeking only the truth. If my desires are rash, then make them disappear, for these desires are the greatest martyrdom to me. However, I feel, O Jesus, that after having aspired to the most lofty heights of Love, if one day I am not to attain them, I feel that I shall have tasted more sweetness in my martyrdom and my folly than I shall taste in the bosom of the joy of the Fatherland, unless you take away the memory of these earthly hopes through a miracle. Allow me, then, during my exile, the delights of love. Allow me to taste the sweet bitterness of my martyrdom.

Jesus, O Jesus, if the desire of loving you is so delightful, what will it be to possess and enjoy this Love?

How can a soul as imperfect as mine aspire to the possession of the plenitude of Love? O Jesus, my first and only Friend, you whom I love uniquely, explain this mystery to me! Why do you not reserve these great aspirations for great souls, for the eagles that soar in the heights?

I look upon myself as a weak little bird, with only a light down as covering. I am not an eagle, but I have only an eagle's eyes and heart. In spite of my extreme littleness I still dare to gaze upon the divine Sun, the Sun of Love, and my heart feels within it all the aspirations of an eagle.

*- SAINT THÉRÈSE OF LISIEUX*

*Saint Thérèse of Lisieux († 1897) was declared a Doctor of the Church in 1997.*

## Faith to See Beyond Appearances

**I**f we live by faith we shall judge things very differently from the way people do who rely only on the evidence of their senses and so remain unaware of the priceless treasure hidden under appearances. If we know that someone in disguise is really our king we shall behave very differently toward him than will someone who sees only an ordinary man. He will treat him as such. Now, if we see the will of God in the most trifling affairs, in every misfortune, and in every disaster, we shall accept them all with an equal joy, delight, and respect. What others fear and flee from, we shall welcome with open doors. The clothing is shabby and mean to the ordinary eye, but we shall respect the royal majesty hidden under it and feel a deepening of our love the more hidden and abject our king is.

I cannot describe what the heart feels when it accepts the divine will so apparently diminished in power, so humble, and so pitiful. How profoundly moved Mary's loving heart was when she saw the poverty of her God lying whimpering and trembling on a bundle of hay in the manger! If we could ask the people of Bethlehem what they thought of this Child, we know what answer we should get. Yet, had he been born in a palace surrounded with all the trapping of a prince, they would have rushed to pay him honor. But let us ask Mary, Joseph, the Magi, and the shepherds, and they will tell us that in this utter poverty they find something indescribable which increases the glory of God and his attractiveness. Paradoxically, what we cannot experience by our senses stimulates, increases, and enriches our faith. The less we see, the more we believe.

*- FATHER JEAN-PIERRE DE CAUSSADE, S.J.*

*Father de Caussade († 1751) was a French Jesuit priest, a writer, and a revered spiritual director.*

### Yes, Jesus, I Love You

How happy Jesus makes me! How sweet is his spirit! I can do nothing but weep and repeat: Jesus, my food!… He continues to love me and to draw me closer to himself. He has forgotten my sins and one would say that he remembers only his own mercy. Each morning he comes into my poor heart and pours out all the effusions of his goodness. I would like, if it were in my power, to wash with my blood those places in which I committed so many sins, where I scandalized so many people. But praised be the mercy of Jesus!

Jesus asks me almost all the time for love, and my heart rather than my lips answers him: "O my Jesus, I wish…" and then I cannot continue. But in the end I exclaim: "Yes, Jesus, I love you; at this moment it seems to me that I love you and I also feel the need to love you more; but, Jesus, I have no more love left in my heart; you know that I have given it all to you. If you want more love, take this heart of mine and fill it with your love, then command me to love and I shall not refuse. I beg you to do this; I desire it."

*- Saint Pius of Pietrelcina*

*Saint Pius of Pietrelcina († 1968) was an Italian Capuchin priest who during his lifetime enjoyed a vast reputation for sanctity.*

### You Are Precious to Jesus

Jesus wants me to tell you again…how much love he has for each one of you— beyond all you can imagine. I worry some of you still have not really met Jesus—one to one—you and Jesus alone. We may spend time in chapel—but have you seen with the eyes of your soul how he looks at you with love? Do you really know the living Jesus—not from books but from being with him in your heart? Have you heard the loving words he speaks to you? Ask for the grace; he is longing to give it. Until you can hear Jesus in the silence of your own heart, you will not be able to hear him saying "I thirst" in the hearts of the poor. Never give up this daily intimate contact with Jesus as the real living person—not just the idea. How can we last even one day without hearing Jesus say, "I love you"—impossible. Our soul needs that as much as the body needs to breathe the air. If not, prayer is dead—meditation only thinking. Jesus wants you each to hear him—speaking in the silence of your heart.

Be careful of all that can block that personal contact with the living Jesus. The devil may try to use the hurts of life, and sometimes our own mistakes—to make you feel it is impossible that Jesus really loves you, is really cleaving to you. This is a danger for all of us. And so sad, because it is completely opposite of what Jesus is really wanting, waiting to tell you. Not only that he loves you, but even more—he longs for you. He misses you when you don't come close. He thirsts for you. He loves you always, even when you don't feel worthy.

When not accepted by others, even by yourself sometimes—he is the one who always accepts you. My children, you don't have to be different for Jesus to love you. Only believe—you are precious to him. Bring all you are suffering to his feet—only open your heart to be loved by him as you are. He will do the rest.

*- SAINT TERESA OF CALCUTTA*

*Saint Teresa of Calcutta († 1997) founded the Missionaries of Charity and won the Nobel Peace Prize.*

## *The Holy Spirit and the Eucharist*

The humanity of Jesus has remained with us in the Holy Eucharist; in that mystery of love Jesus accomplishes his unparalleled marvels in souls, and all operations of grace through the other sacraments are irradiations of that mystery, which in the Church is the center not only of her worship, but of her life and sanctity.

The Holy Spirit and the Eucharist have divine connections; both mysteries are fountains of purity and of life, but not two separated fountains; united by an inexpressible harmony, they form but one and the same fountain. Therefore, although the sacrament of love was instituted on the eve of the Passion, it was not dispensed in the Church until Pentecost. On that day the heavenly fountain, united with that of earth, would pour throughout the world the holy inundation of purity; when the Holy Spirit, the eternal perfecter, would complete all that Jesus had established, which, like holy seeds, needed to be watered by power from on high in order to germinate....

The Eucharist is the fountain of purity; souls and bodies are sanctified with the ineffable contact of the most holy humanity of Jesus.... The wisdom of God, who disposes all things with wonderful sweetness, desires that the divine reflection of purity pass through the virginal Flesh and the precious Blood of Jesus, which are flesh of our flesh and blood of our blood.

By the ineffable contact of the Holy Eucharist even the mysterious seed of the resurrection is deposited in our lowly flesh. This, after all, is the perfection, as it were, of purity of the body because it is the plenitude of its divinization.

The Eucharist, the mystery through which Jesus spreads himself out, so to speak, because he goes to all places and passes through all ages and enters all souls who wish to receive him, is also an effusion of purity.

Someone has said that a single surge of either love or of suffering can save the world; the Holy Spirit and the Eucharist envelop the world in those two waves because the Holy Spirit and the Eucharist both come from Calvary and they extend upon the earth the empire of the cross formed with love and suffering.

*- SERVANT OF GOD LUIS MARÍA MARTÍNEZ*

*Archbishop Martínez († 1956) was a spiritual author and the first official Primate of Mexico.*

## *O Boundless Charity!*

O eternal Trinity! Eternal Trinity! O fire and deep well of charity! O you who are madly in love with your creature! O eternal truth! O eternal fire! O eternal wisdom given for our redemption! But did your wisdom come into the world alone? No. For wisdom was not separate from power, nor was power without mercy. You, wisdom, did not come alone then, but the whole

Trinity was there. O eternal Trinity, mad with love, of what use to you was our redemption? None at all, for you have no need of us, you who are our God. For whose good was it? Only humanity's.

O boundless charity! Just as you gave us yourself, wholly God and wholly human, so you left us all of yourself as food so that while we are pilgrims in this life we might not collapse in our weariness but be strengthened by you, heavenly food. O mercenary people! And what has your God left you? He has left you himself, wholly God and wholly human, hidden under the whiteness of this bread.

O fire of love! Was it not enough to gift us with creation in your image and likeness, and to create us anew to grace in your Son's blood, without giving us yourself as food, the whole of divine being, the whole of God? What drove you? Nothing but your charity, mad with love as you are!

And just as you did not send the Word alone as gift for our redemption, so you left us not him alone as food, but, as I have said, the whole divine being, as one mad with love for your creature. Even more—just as you did not leave us only yourself as food, so you do not give only yourself to the soul who turns her back on herself completely for love of you and desires and seeks only the glory and praise of your name. To such as these you do not give just yourself. No, you make them strong in your own power against the devil's assaults, against other people's abuse, against the rebelliousness of their own flesh, against all anguish and trouble from whatever source it may come. You enlighten them with your Son's wisdom to know both themselves and your truth as well as the devil's secret deceits. And you set their hearts ablaze with the Holy Spirit's fire, with desire to love and follow you in truth.

*- SAINT CATHERINE OF SIENA*

*Saint Catherine of Siena († 1380), Doctor of the Church, was a Dominican, stigmatist, and papal counselor.*

# Prayers and Devotions

## Anima Christi

Soul of Christ, sanctify me.
Body of Christ, save me.
Blood of Christ, embolden me.
Water from the side of Christ, wash me.
Passion of Christ, strengthen me.
O good Jesus, hear me.
Within your wounds hide me.
Never permit me to be parted from you.
From the evil Enemy defend me.
At the hour of my death call me
and bid me come to you,
that with your Saints I may praise you
for age upon age.
Amen.

## Suscipe

Receive, Lord, my entire freedom.
Accept the whole of my memory,
my intellect and my will.
Whatever I have or possess,
it was you who gave it to me;
I restore it to you in full,
and I surrender it completely
to the guidance of your will.
Give me only love of you
together with your grace,
and I am rich enough
and ask for nothing more.
Amen.

## Prayer to
## Our Lord Jesus Christ Crucified

Behold, O good and loving Jesus,
that I cast myself on my knees before you
and, with the greatest fervor of spirit,
I pray and beseech you to instill into my heart
ardent sentiments of faith, hope and charity,
with true repentance for my sins
and a most firm purpose of amendment.
With deep affection and sorrow
I ponder intimately
and contemplate in my mind your five wounds,
having before my eyes what the prophet David
had already put in your mouth about yourself,
    O good Jesus:
They have pierced my hands and my feet;
they have numbered all my bones (Ps 22:17-18).

## The Universal Prayer
## attributed to Pope Clement XI

I believe, O Lord, but may I believe more firmly;
I hope, but may I hope more securely;
I love, but may I love more ardently;
I sorrow, but may I sorrow more deeply.

I adore you as my first beginning;
I long for you as my last end;
I praise you as my constant benefactor;
I invoke you as my gracious protector.

By your wisdom direct me,
by your righteousness restrain me,

by your indulgence console me,
by your power protect me.

I offer you, Lord, my thoughts to be directed to you,
my words, to be about you,
my deeds, to respect your will,
my trials, to be endured for you.

I will whatever you will,
I will it because you will it,
I will it in the way you will it,
I will it for as long as you will it.

Lord, enlighten my understanding, I pray:
arouse my will,
cleanse my heart,
sanctify my soul.

May I weep for past sins,
repel future temptations,
correct evil inclinations,
nurture appropriate virtues.

Give me, good God,
love for you, hatred for myself,
zeal for my neighbor,
contempt for the world.

May I strive to obey superiors,
to help those dependent on me,
to have care for my friends,
forgiveness for my enemies.

May I conquer sensuality by austerity,
avarice by generosity,
anger by gentleness,
lukewarmness by fervor.

Render me prudent in planning,
steadfast in dangers,
patient in adversity,
humble in prosperity.

Make me, O Lord, attentive at prayer,
moderate at meals,
diligent in work,
steadfast in intent.

May I be careful to maintain interior innocence,
outward modesty,
exemplary behavior,
a regular life.

May I be always watchful in subduing nature,
in nourishing grace,
in observing your law,
in winning salvation.

May I learn from you
how precarious are earthly things,
how great divine things,
how fleeting is time,
how lasting things eternal.

Grant that I may prepare for death,
fear judgment,
flee hell,
gain paradise.
Through Christ our Lord. Amen.

## Obsecro Te

I beseech thee, most sweet Lord Jesus Christ, grant that thy Passion may be to me a power by which I may be strengthened, protected and defended. May thy wounds be to me food and drink, by which I may be nourished, inebriated and overjoyed. May the sprinkling of thy Blood be to me an ablution for all my sins. May thy death prove to me life everlasting, and thy Cross be to me an eternal glory. In these be my refreshment, my joy, my preservation and sweetness of heart. Who livest and reignest world without end. Amen.

## Prayer of St. Bonaventure

Pierce, O most sweet Lord Jesus, my inmost soul with the most joyous and healthful wound of thy love, and with true, calm and most holy apostolic charity, that my soul may ever languish and melt with entire love and longing for thee, may yearn for thee and for thy courts, may long to be dissolved and to be with thee.

Grant that my soul may hunger after thee, the Bread of Angels, the refreshment of holy souls, our daily and supersubstantial bread, having all sweetness and savor and every delightful taste. May my heart ever hunger after and feed upon thee, whom the angels desire to look upon, and may my inmost soul be filled with the sweetness of thy savor; may it ever thirst for thee, the fountain of life, the fountain of wisdom and knowledge, the fountain of eternal light, the torrent of pleasure, the fullness of the house of God; may it ever compass thee, seek thee, find thee, run to thee, come up to thee, meditate on thee, speak of thee, and do all for the praise and glory of thy name, with humility and discretion, with love and delight, with ease and affection, with perseverance to the end; and be thou alone ever my hope, my entire confidence, my riches, my delight, my pleasure, my joy, my rest and tranquility, my peace, my sweetness, my food, my refreshment, my refuge, my help, my wisdom, my portion, my possession, my treasure; in whom may my mind and my heart be ever fixed and firm and rooted immovably. **Amen.**

## O Sacrum Convivium

O Sacred Banquet, in which Christ becomes our food, the memory of his passion is celebrated, the soul is filled with grace, and a pledge of future glory is given to us.

## O Bone Iesu

O good Jesus! O most sweet Jesus! O Jesus, Son of the Virgin Mary, full of mercy and tenderness! O sweet Jesus! according to thy great mercy have mercy on me. O most merciful Jesus! I implore thee by the Precious Blood which thou didst deign to shed for sinners, to wash away my iniquities, and look upon me in my misery and unworthiness, humbly begging pardon, and calling upon this holy name, Jesus. O name of Jesus, name of sweetness! Name of Jesus, name of delights. Name of Jesus, name of comfort. For, what is Jesus but Savior? Therefore, Jesus, on account of thy holy name, be to me a Jesus, and save me.

## Salutation to Our Lord Jesus Christ

Hail, Christ's Body, born of the holy Virgin,
Living flesh, perfect Godhead, true man.

Hail, true salvation, strength, life,
 redemption of the world,
May your right hand free us from all evils.

Hail, Christ's Blood, most holy drink of heaven,
Saving flood, washing away our sins.

Hail, Blood sprinkled from the wound
   in Christ's side,
Hail, saving flood, hanging on the Cross.

## Salve, Salutaris Victima

Hail, saving victim, offered on the gibbet of the Cross for me and for the whole human race. Hail, precious Blood, flowing from the wounds of our crucified Lord Jesus Christ and washing away the sins of the whole world. Remember, O Lord, thy creature which thou hast redeemed by thy precious Blood. Amen.

## Prayer to our Lord Jesus Christ

Look down upon me, good and gentle Jesus, while before thy face I humbly kneel, and with burning soul pray and beseech thee to fix deep in my heart lively sentiments of faith, hope, and charity, true contrition for my sins, and a firm purpose of amendment; the while I contemplate with great love and tender pity thy five wounds, pondering over them within me, whilst I call to mind what the Prophet David put in thy mouth concerning thee, O good Jesus: "They have dug my hands and feet; they have numbered all my bones."

## Domine Iesu Christe, qui neminem vis perire

### (Lord Jesus Christ, You Will That None Should Perish)

Lord Jesus Christ, you will that none should perish, and to you no prayer is ever made without hope of mercy, for you have said with your holy and blessed lips: All things whatsoever you ask for in my name, shall be done to you. And so I ask you, Lord, for the sake of your holy name, to grant me at the moment of my death full use of my faculties with the ability to speak, wholehearted sorrow for my sins, true faith, well-ordered hope and perfect charity, that I may say to you with a pure heart: Into your hands, O Lord, I commend my spirit, for you have redeemed me, God of truth, who are blessed for ever and ever. Amen.

## Domine Iesu, Noverim Me

O Lord Jesus, let me know myself, let me know thee
And desire nothing else but only thee.
Let me hate myself and love thee;
And do all things for the sake of thee.

Let me humble myself, and exalt thee,
And think of nothing but only of thee.
Let me die to myself, and live in thee,
And take whatever happens as coming from thee.

Let me forsake myself and walk after thee;
And ever desire to follow thee.
Let me flee from myself, and turn to thee;
That so I may merit to be defended by thee.

Let me fear for myself, let me fear thee:
And be amongst those who are chosen by thee.

Let me distrust myself, and trust in thee,
And ever obey for the love of thee.

Let me cleave to nothing but only to thee,
And ever be poor for the sake of thee.
Look upon me, that I may love thee;
Call me, that I may see thee
And forever possess thee. Amen.

# LITANIES

## Litany of the Sacred Heart of Jesus

Lord, have mercy.
*Lord, have mercy.*
Christ, have mercy.
*Christ, have mercy.*
Lord, have mercy.
*Lord, have mercy.*
God our Father in heaven,
*have mercy on us.*
God the Son, Redeemer of the world,
*have mercy on us.*
God the Holy Spirit,
*have mercy on us.*
Holy Trinity, one God,
*have mercy on us.*
Heart of Jesus, Son of the eternal Father,
*have mercy on us.*
Heart of Jesus, formed by the Holy Spirit in
the womb of the Virgin Mother,
*have mercy on us.*
Heart of Jesus, one with the eternal Word,
*have mercy on us.*
Heart of Jesus, infinite in majesty,
*have mercy on us.*
Heart of Jesus, holy temple of God,
*have mercy on us.*
Heart of Jesus, tabernacle of the Most High,
*have mercy on us.*

Heart of Jesus, house of God and gate of heaven,
*have mercy on us.*

Heart of Jesus, aflame with love for us,
*have mercy on us.*

Heart of Jesus, source of justice and love,
*have mercy on us.*

Heart of Jesus, full of goodness and love,
*have mercy on us.*

Heart of Jesus, wellspring of all virtue,
*have mercy on us.*

Heart of Jesus, worthy of all praise,
*have mercy on us.*

Heart of Jesus, King and center of all hearts,
*have mercy on us.*

Heart of Jesus, treasure-house of wisdom
and knowledge,
*have mercy on us.*

Heart of Jesus, in whom there dwells the
fullness of God,
*have mercy on us.*

Heart of Jesus, in whom the Father is well pleased,
*have mercy on us.*

Heart of Jesus, from whose fullness we
have all received,
*have mercy on us.*

Heart of Jesus, desire of the eternal hills,
*have mercy on us.*

Heart of Jesus, patient and full of mercy,
*have mercy on us.*

Heart of Jesus, generous to all who turn to you,
*have mercy on us.*

Heart of Jesus, fountain of life and holiness,
*have mercy on us.*

Heart of Jesus, atonement for our sins,
*have mercy on us.*

Heart of Jesus, overwhelmed with insults,
*have mercy on us.*

Heart of Jesus, broken for our sins,
*have mercy on us.*

Heart of Jesus, obedient even to death,
*have mercy on us.*

Heart of Jesus, pierced by a lance,
*have mercy on us.*

Heart of Jesus, source of all consolation,
*have mercy on us.*

Heart of Jesus, our life and resurrection,
*have mercy on us.*

Heart of Jesus, our peace and reconciliation,
*have mercy on us.*

Heart of Jesus, victim of our sins,
*have mercy on us.*

Heart of Jesus, salvation of all who trust in you,
*have mercy on us.*

Heart of Jesus, hope of all who die in you,
*have mercy on us.*

Heart of Jesus, delight of all the saints,
*have mercy on us.*

Lamb of God, you take away the sins of the world,
*have mercy on us.*

Lamb of God, you take away the sins of the world,
*have mercy on us.*

Lamb of God, you take away the sins of the world,
*have mercy on us.*

Jesus, gentle and humble of heart.
*Touch our hearts and make them like your own.*

Let us pray.

Father, we rejoice in the gifts of love we have received from the Heart of Jesus your Son. Open our hearts to share his life and continue to bless us with his love. We ask this in the name of Jesus the Lord. **Amen.**

## Litany of the Most Precious Blood

Lord, have mercy.
*Lord, have mercy.*

Christ, have mercy.
*Christ, have mercy.*

Lord, have mercy.
*Lord, have mercy.*

God our Father in heaven,
*have mercy on us.*

God the Son, Redeemer of the world,
*have mercy on us.*

God the Holy Spirit,
*have mercy on us.*

Holy Trinity, one God,
*have mercy on us.*

Blood of Christ, only Son of the Father,
*save us.*

Blood of Christ, Incarnate Word,
*save us.*

Blood of Christ, of the new and eternal covenant,
*save us.*

Blood of Christ, that spilled to the ground,
*save us.*

Blood of Christ, that flowed at the scourging,
*save us.*

Blood of Christ, dripping from the thorns,
*save us.*

Blood of Christ, shed on the Cross,
*save us.*

Blood of Christ, the price of our redemption,
*save us.*

Blood of Christ, our only claim to pardon,
*save us.*

Blood of Christ, our blessing cup,
*save us.*

Blood of Christ, in which we are washed,
*save us.*

Blood of Christ, torrent of mercy,
*save us.*

Blood of Christ, that overcomes evil,
*save us.*

Blood of Christ, strength of the martyrs,
*save us.*

Blood of Christ, endurance of the saints,
*save us.*

Blood of Christ, that makes the barren fruitful,
*save us.*

Blood of Christ, protection of the threatened,
*save us.*

Blood of Christ, comfort of the weary,
*save us.*

Blood of Christ, solace of the mourner,
*save us.*

Blood of Christ, hope of the repentant,
*save us.*

Blood of Christ, consolation of the dying,
   *save us.*

Blood of Christ, our peace and refreshment,
   *save us.*

Blood of Christ, our pledge of life,
   *save us.*

Blood of Christ, by which we pass to glory,
   *save us.*

Blood of Christ, most worthy of honor,
   *save us.*

Lamb of God, you take away the sins of the world,
   *have mercy on us.*

Lamb of God, you take away the sins of the world,
   *have mercy on us.*

Lamb of God, you take away the sins of the world,
   *have mercy on us.*

Lord, you redeemed us by your Blood.
   *You have made us a Kingdom to serve our God.*

Let us pray.

Father, by the Blood of your Son you have set us free and saved us from death. Continue your work of love within us, that by constantly celebrating the mystery of our salvation we may reach the eternal life it promises. We ask this through Christ our Lord. **Amen.**

## A Litany of Trust

From the belief that I have to earn your love,
*Deliver me, Jesus.*

From the fear that I am unlovable,
*Deliver me, Jesus.*

From the false security that I have what it takes,
*Deliver me, Jesus.*

From the fear that trusting you
will leave me more destitute,
*Deliver me, Jesus.*

From all suspicion of your words and promises,
*Deliver me, Jesus.*

From the rebellion against childlike
dependency on you,
*Deliver me, Jesus.*

From refusals and reluctances in accepting your will,
*Deliver me, Jesus.*

From anxiety about the future,
*Deliver me, Jesus.*

From resentment or excessive
preoccupation with the past,
*Deliver me, Jesus.*

From restless self-seeking in the present moment,
*Deliver me, Jesus.*

From disbelief in your love and presence,
*Deliver me, Jesus.*

From the fear of being asked
   to give more than I have,
      *Deliver me, Jesus.*

From the belief that my life
   has no meaning or worth,
      *Deliver me, Jesus.*

From the fear of what love demands,
      *Deliver me, Jesus.*

From discouragement,
      *Deliver me, Jesus.*

That you are continually holding me,
   sustaining me, loving me,
      *Jesus, I trust in you.*

That your love goes deeper than my sins and failings
   and transforms me,
      *Jesus, I trust in you.*

That not knowing what tomorrow brings
   is an invitation to lean on you,
      *Jesus, I trust in you.*

That you are with me in my suffering,
      *Jesus, I trust in you.*

That my suffering, united to your own,
   will bear fruit in this life and the next,
      *Jesus, I trust in you.*

That you will not leave me an orphan,
   that you are present in your Church,
      *Jesus, I trust in you.*

That your plan is better than anything else,
*Jesus, I trust in you.*

That you always hear me and in your goodness
always respond to me,
*Jesus, I trust in you.*

That you give me the grace to accept forgiveness
and to forgive others,
*Jesus, I trust in you.*

That you give me all the strength I need
for what is asked,
*Jesus, I trust in you.*

That my life is a gift,
*Jesus, I trust in you.*

That you will teach me to trust you,
*Jesus, I trust in you.*

That you are my Lord and my God,
*Jesus, I trust in you.*

That I am your beloved one,
*Jesus, I trust in you.*

– SISTER FAUSTINA MARIA PIA, S.V.

## A "Magnificat with Mary" Litany

*Composed by the Sisters of Life*

Mary has been referred to as the first and original Monstrance. With the Son of God in her womb, our Lady carried Christ wherever she went. When she was praised by her cousin Elizabeth at the Visitation, Mary sang her own song of praise to God, the *Magnificat*. The dazzling beauty of the Mother of God, like a shiny, golden monstrance, invites us to look upon and adore her divine Son. In marveling at her fullness of grace, we are drawn to marvel at the Source of Grace, the Incarnate Word. In praying the following litany before the Blessed Sacrament—the Body, Blood, Soul, and Divinity of our Lord Jesus Christ—we unite ourselves to our Lady, Mother of Christ and Mother of Adorers. And through her, we are united to Jesus.

– FR. SEBASTIAN WHITE, O.P.

Mary, with your consent to become the Mother of God, torrents of grace poured forth upon the earth, opening up for me a path to follow.

In times of loneliness,
*Mary, be with me.*

In times of turmoil and uncertainty,
*Mary, be with me.*

In times of grief, loss, or illness,
*Mary, be with me.*

In times of sadness or depression,
*Mary, be with me.*

In times of lost plans and broken promises,
*Mary, be with me.*

When I am anxious about the welfare of my family,
*Mary, be with me.*

When a job or financial stress
weighs heavily on my heart,
*Mary, be with me.*

When I am discouraged by the weight of my sins,
*Mary, be with me.*

When I am tempted,
*Mary, be with me.*

When I am afraid,
*Mary, be with me.*

When the Lord calls me to greater kindness and love,
*Mary, be with me.*

When the Lord calls me to greater forgiveness,
*Mary, be with me.*

When the Lord calls me to greater purity,
*Mary, be with me.*

*On the wings of your* Fiat, *Mary, I proclaim
mine. Together we sing a* Magnificat *of praise:*

For all the blessings in my life,
*I praise you, Jesus.*

For the gift of today,
*I praise you, Jesus.*

For the gift of loved ones,
*I praise you, Jesus.*

For the gift of my life,
*I praise you, Jesus.*

For creating me with a special purpose and plan,
*I praise you, Jesus.*

For never giving up on me,
*I praise you, Jesus.*

For your infinite love,
*I praise you, Jesus.*

For never leaving me,
*I praise you, Jesus.*

For your inexhaustible mercy,
*I praise you, Jesus.*

For laying down your life for me,
*I praise you, Jesus.*

For your presence in the Eucharist,
*I praise you, Jesus.*


*For the greater good you will bring out of everything, especially:*

In moments when I feel helpless and vulnerable,
*I praise you, Jesus.*

In the midst of uncertainty,
*I praise you, Jesus.*

In the midst of humiliation,
*I praise you, Jesus.*

In the midst of difficulty,
*I praise you, Jesus.*

In the midst of what appears as failure,
*I praise you, Jesus.*

For sending your Mother to me
in both joyful and sorrowful moments,
*I praise you, Jesus.*

With Mary I sing:
*The Almighty has done great things
for me, and holy is his Name. Amen.*

# EUCHARISTIC HYMNS

## Adoremus in Aeternum

Ant. *Let us adore forever the Most Holy Sacrament.*

Praise the Lord, all ye nations: praise him, all ye people.

Because his mercy is confirmed upon us: and the truth of the Lord remaineth forever.

Glory be to the Father, and to the Son, and to the Holy Spirit.

As it was in the beginning, is now, and ever shall be, world without end. Amen.

Ant. *Let us adore forever the Most Holy Sacrament.*

## Adoro Te Devote

(translated by Gerard Manley Hopkins, s.j.)

Godhead here in hiding, whom I do adore,
Masked by these bare shadows, shape
   and nothing more,
See Lord, at thy service low lies here a heart
Lost, all lost in wonder at the God thou art.

Seeing, touching, tasting are in thee deceived:
How says trusty hearing? that shall be believed;

What God's Son has told me, take for truth I do;
Truth himself speaks truly or there's nothing true.

On the cross thy godhead made no sign to men,
Here thy very manhood steals from human ken:
Both are my confession, both are my belief,
And I pray the prayer of the dying thief.

I am not like Thomas, wounds I cannot see,
But can plainly call thee Lord and God as he;
Let me to a deeper faith daily nearer move,
Daily make me harder hope and dearer love.

O thou our reminder of Christ crucified,
Living Bread, the life of us from whom he died,
Lend this life to me then: feed and feast my mind,
There be thou the sweetness man was meant to find.

Bring the tender tale true of the Pelican;
Bathe me, Jesu Lord, in what thy bosom ran—
Blood whereof a single drop has power to win
All the world forgiveness of its world of sin.

Jesu, whom I look at shrouded here below,
I beseech thee send me what I thirst for so,
Some day to gaze on thee face to face in light
And be blest for ever with thy glory's sight. Amen.

## Ave Verum Corpus Natum

Body of Jesus,
born of the Virgin Mary,
body bowed in agony,

and offered for us in sacrifice,
body pierced and flowing
with blood and water,
come at the hour of our death
as our living bread,
the foretaste of eternal glory:
come, Lord Jesus,
loving and gracious Son of Mary.

## Iesu, Dulcis Memoria

Jesu, the very thought of thee,
with sweetness fills my breast,
but sweeter far thy face to see,
and in thy presence rest.

Nor voice can sing, nor heart can frame,
nor can the memory find
a sweeter sound than thy blest name,
O Savior of mankind!

O hope of every contrite heart
O joy of all the meek,
to those who fall, how kind thou art!
how good to those who seek!

But what to those who find? Ah this
nor tongue nor pen can show:
the love of Jesus, what it is
none but his loved ones know.

Jesu, our only joy be thou,
As thou our prize wilt be:

Jesu, be thou our glory now,
And through eternity.
Amen.

### Lauda, Sion

Laud, O Zion, your salvation,
Laud with hymns of exultation,
Christ, your king and shepherd true:

Bring him all the praise you know,
He is more than you bestow.
Never can you reach his due.

Special theme for glad thanksgiving
Is the quick'ning and the living
Bread today before you set:

From his hands of old partaken,
As we know, by faith unshaken,
Where the Twelve at supper met.

Full and clear ring out your chanting,
Joy nor sweetest grace be wanting,
From your heart let praises burst:

For today the feast is holden,
When the institution olden,
Of that supper was rehearsed.

Here the new law's new oblation,
By the new king's revelation,
Ends the form of ancient rite:

Now the new the old effaces,
Truth away the shadow chases,
 Light dispels the gloom of night.

What he did at supper seated,
Christ ordained to be repeated,
 His memorial ne'er to cease:

And his rule for guidance taking,
Bread and wine we hallow, making
 Thus our sacrifice of peace.

This the truth each Christian learns,
Bread into his flesh he turns,
 To his precious blood the wine:

Sight has fail'd, nor thought conceives,
But a dauntless faith believes,
 Resting on a pow'r divine.

Here beneath these signs are hidden
Priceless things to sense forbidden;
 Sign, not things are all we see:

Blood is poured and flesh is broken,
Yet in either wondrous token
 Christ entire we know to be.

Whoso of this food partakes,
Does not rend the Lord nor breaks;
 Christ is whole to all that tastes:

Thousands are, as one, receivers,
One, as thousands of believers,
 Eats of him who cannot waste.

Bad and good the feast are sharing,
Of what divers dooms preparing,
 Endless death, or endless life.

Life to these, to those damnation,
See how like participation
    Is with unlike issues rife.

When the sacrament is broken,
Doubt not, but believe 'tis spoken,
    That each sever'd outward token
        doth the very whole contain.

Nought the precious gift divides,
Breaking but the sign betides
    Jesus still the same abides,
        still unbroken does remain.

Lo! the angel's food is given
To the pilgrim who has striven;
    See the children's bread from heaven,
        which on dogs may not be spent.

Truth the ancient types fulfilling,
Isaac bound, a victim willing,
    Paschal lamb, its lifeblood spilling,
        manna to the fathers sent.

Very bread, good shepherd, tend us,
Jesu, of your love befriend us,
    You refresh us, you defend us,
    Your eternal goodness send us
In the land of life to see.

You who all things can and know,
Who on earth such food bestow,
    Grant us with your saints, though lowest,
    Where the heav'nly feast you show,
Fellow heirs and guests to be. Amen. Alleluia.

## O Salutaris Hostia

O Saving Victim! opening wide
The gate of Heaven to man below!
Our foes press on from every side;
Thine aid supply, thy strength bestow.

To Thy great Name be endless praise,
Immortal Godhead! One in Three!
O grant us endless length of days
In our true native land with Thee!

## Pange, Lingua

Sing, my tongue, the Savior's glory,
of his flesh the mystery sing;
of the blood, all price exceeding,
shed by our immortal King,
destined, for the world's redemption,
from a noble womb to spring.

Of a pure and spotless Virgin
born for us on earth below,
he, as Man, with man conversing,
stayed, the seeds of truth to sow;
then he closed in solemn order,
wondrously his life of woe.

On the night of that Last Supper,
seated with his chosen band,
he the Paschal victim eating,
first fulfills the Law's command;

then as Food to his Apostles
gives himself with his own hand.

Word-made-Flesh, the bread of nature
by his word to Flesh he turns;
wine into His Blood he changes;-
what though sense no change discerns?
Only be the heart in earnest,
faith her lesson quickly learns.

Down in adoration falling,
Lo! the sacred Host we hail;
Lo! o'er ancient forms departing,
newer rites of grace prevail;
faith for all defects supplying,
where the feeble senses fail.

To the everlasting Father,
and the Son who reigns on high,
with the Holy Ghost proceeding
forth from each eternally,
be salvation, honor, blessing,
might and endless majesty.
Amen. Alleluia.

# ADDITIONAL SCRIPTURE READINGS

## GOSPEL PASSAGES 〰〰〰〰〰〰〰〰〰〰〰〰〰〰〰〰〰

### Matthew 11:25-30

*I am gentle and humble of heart.*

A T THAT TIME Jesus said in reply, "I give praise to you, Father, Lord of heaven and earth, for although you have hidden these things from the wise and the learned you have revealed them to the childlike. Yes, Father, such has been your gracious will. All things have been handed over to me by my Father. No one knows the Son except the Father, and no one knows the Father except the Son and anyone to whom the Son wishes to reveal him.

"Come to me, all you who labor and are burdened, and I will give you rest. Take my yoke upon you and learn from me, for I am meek and humble of heart; and you will find rest for yourselves. For my yoke is easy, and my burden light."

### Luke 15:1-10

*Heaven is filled with joy when one sinner turns back to God.*

T HE TAX COLLECTORS and sinners were all drawing near to listen to him, but the Pharisees and scribes began to complain, saying, "This man welcomes sinners and eats with them." So to them he addressed this parable. "What man among you having a hundred sheep and losing one of them would not leave the ninety-nine in the desert and go after the lost one until he finds it? And when he does find it, he sets it on his shoulders with great joy and, upon his arrival home, he calls together his friends and neighbors and says to them, 'Rejoice with me because I have found my lost sheep.' I tell you, in just the same way there will be more joy in heaven over one sinner who repents than over ninety-nine righteous people who have no need of repentance.

"Or what woman having ten coins and losing one would not light a lamp and sweep the house, searching carefully until she finds it? And when she does find it, she calls together her friends and neighbors and says to them, 'Rejoice with me because I have found the coin that I lost.' In just the same way, I tell you, there will be rejoicing among the angels of God over one sinner who repents."

## Luke 15:1-3, 11-32

*We are celebrating because your brother has come back from death.*

THE TAX COLLECTORS and sinners were all drawing near to listen to him, but the Pharisees and scribes began to complain, saying, "This man welcomes sinners and eats with them." So to them he addressed this parable.

"A man had two sons, and the younger son said to his father, 'Father, give me the share of your estate that should come to me.' So the father divided the property between them. After a few days, the younger son collected all his belongings and set off to a distant country where he squandered his inheritance on a life of dissipation. When he had freely spent everything, a severe famine struck that country, and he found himself in dire need. So he hired himself out to one of the local citizens who sent him to his farm to tend the swine. And he longed to eat his fill of the pods on which the swine fed, but nobody gave him any. Coming to his senses he thought, 'How many of my father's hired workers have more than enough food to eat, but here am I, dying from hunger. I shall get up and go to my father and I shall say to him, "Father, I have sinned against heaven and against you. I no longer deserve to be called your son; treat me as you would treat one of your hired workers."' So he got up and went back to his father. While he was still a long way off, his father caught sight of him, and was filled with compassion. He ran to his son, embraced him and kissed him. His son said to him, 'Father, I have sinned against heaven and against you; I no longer deserve to be called your son.' But his father ordered his servants, 'Quickly bring the finest robe and put it on him; put a ring on his finger and sandals on his feet. Take the fattened calf and slaughter it. Then let us celebrate with a feast, because this son of mine was dead, and has come to life again; he was lost, and has been found.' Then the celebration began. Now the older son had been out in the field and, on his way back, as he neared the house, he heard the sound of music and dancing. He called one of the servants and asked what this might mean. The servant said to him, 'Your brother has returned and your father has slaughtered the fattened calf because he has him back safe and sound.' He became angry, and when he refused to enter the house, his father came out and pleaded with him. He said to his father in reply, 'Look, all these years I served you and not once did I disobey your orders; yet you never gave me even a young goat to feast on with my friends. But when your son returns who swallowed up your property with prostitutes, for him you slaughter the fattened calf.' He said to him, 'My son, you are here with me always; everything I have is yours. But now we must celebrate and rejoice, because your brother was dead and has come to life again; he was lost and has been found.'"

## John 10:11-18

*A good shepherd is ready to die for his flock.*

"I AM THE GOOD SHEPHERD. A good shepherd lays down his life for the sheep. A hired man, who is not a shepherd and whose sheep are not his own, sees a wolf coming and leaves the sheep and runs away, and the wolf catches and scatters them. This is because he works for pay and has no concern for the sheep. I am the good shepherd, and I know mine and mine know me, just as the Father knows me and I know the Father; and I will lay down my life for the sheep. I have other sheep that do not belong to this fold. These also I must lead, and they will hear my voice, and there will be one flock, one shepherd. This is why the Father loves me, because I lay down my life in order to take it up again. No one takes it from me, but I lay it down on my own. I have power to lay it down, and power to take it up again. This command I have received from my Father."

## John 15:1-8

*Live in me as I live in you.*

"I AM THE TRUE VINE, and my Father is the vine grower. He takes away every branch in me that does not bear fruit, and every one that does he prunes so that it bears more fruit. You are already pruned because of the word that I spoke to you. Remain in me, as I remain in you. Just as a branch cannot bear fruit on its own unless it remains on the vine, so neither can you unless you remain in me. I am the vine, you are the branches. Whoever remains in me and I in him will bear much fruit, because without me you can do nothing. Anyone who does not remain in me will be thrown out like a branch and wither; people will gather them and throw them into a fire and they will be burned. If you remain in me and my words remain in you, ask for whatever you want and it will be done for you. By this is my Father glorified, that you bear much fruit and become my disciples."

## John 15:9-17

*Love one another as I love you.*

"As the Father loves me, so I also love you. Remain in my love. If you keep my commandments, you will remain in my love, just as I have kept my Father's commandments and remain in his love.

"I have told you this so that my joy may be in you and your joy may be complete. This is my commandment:

love one another as I love you. No one has greater love than this, to lay down one's life for one's friends. You are my friends if you do what I command you. I no longer call you slaves, because a slave does not know what his master is doing. I have called you friends, because I have told you everything I have heard from my Father. It was not you who chose me, but I who chose you and appointed you to go and bear fruit that will remain, so that whatever you ask the Father in my name he may give you. This I command you: love one another."

## John 17:20-26

*Father, you loved them as you loved me.*

"I PRAY not only for them, but also for those who will believe in me through their word, so that they may all be one, as you, Father, are in me and I in you, that they also may be in us, that the world may believe that you sent me. And I have given them the glory you gave me, so that they may be one, as we are one, I in them and you in me, that they may be brought to perfection as one, that the world may know that you sent me, and that you loved them even as you loved me. Father, they are your gift to me. I wish that where I am they also may be with me, that they may see my glory that you gave me, because you loved me before the foundation of the world. Righteous Father, the world also does not know you, but I know you, and they know that you sent me. I made known to them your name and I will make it known, that the love with which you loved me may be in them and I in them."

John 19:31-37

*When they pierced his side with a spear, blood and water flowed out.*

NOW SINCE IT WAS preparation day, in order that the bodies might not remain on the cross on the sabbath, for the sabbath day of that week was a solemn one, the Jews asked Pilate that their legs be broken and they be taken down. So the soldiers came and broke the legs of the first and then of the other one who was crucified with Jesus. But when they came to Jesus and saw that he was already dead, they did not break his legs, but one soldier thrust his lance into his side, and immediately blood and water flowed out. An eyewitness has testified, and his testimony is true; he knows that he is speaking the truth, so that you also may [come to] believe. For this happened so that the scripture passage might be fulfilled:

"Not a bone of it will be broken."

And again another passage says:

"They will look upon him whom they have pierced."

Mark 14:12-16, 22-26

*This is my body. This is my blood.*

ON THE FIRST DAY of the Feast of Unleavened Bread, when they sacrificed the Passover lamb, his disciples said to him, "Where do you want us to go and prepare for you to eat the Passover?" He sent two of his disciples and said to them, "Go into the city and a man will meet you, carrying a jar of water. Follow him. Wherever he enters, say to the master of the house, 'The Teacher says, "Where is my guest room where I may eat the Passover with my disciples?"' Then he will show you a large upper room furnished and ready. Make the preparations for us there." The disciples then went off, entered the city, and found it just as he had told them; and they prepared the Passover.

While they were eating, he took bread, said the blessing, broke it, and gave it to them, and said, "Take it; this is my body." Then he took a cup, gave thanks, and gave it to them, and they all drank from it. He said to them, "This is my blood of the covenant, which will be shed for many. Amen, I say to you, I shall not drink again the fruit of the vine until the day when I drink it new in the kingdom of God." Then, after singing a hymn, they went out to the Mount of Olives.

## Mark 15:16-20

*They dressed Jesus up in purple and put a crown of thorns on him.*

THE SOLDIERS led him away inside the palace, that is, the praetorium, and assembled the whole cohort. They clothed him in purple and, weaving a crown of thorns, placed it on him. They began to salute him with, "Hail, King of the Jews!" and kept striking his head with a reed and spitting upon him. They knelt before him in homage. And when they had mocked him, they stripped him of the purple cloak, dressed him in his own clothes, and led him out to crucify him.

## Luke 9:11-17

*All the people ate and were satisfied.*

THE CROWDS, meanwhile, learned of this and followed him. He received them and spoke to them about the kingdom of God, and he healed those who needed to be cured. As the day was drawing to a close, the Twelve approached him and said, "Dismiss the crowd so that they can go to the surrounding villages and farms and find lodging and provisions; for we are in a deserted place here." He said to them, "Give them some food yourselves." They replied, "Five loaves and two fish are all we have, unless we ourselves go and buy food for all these people." Now the men there numbered about five thousand. Then he said to his disciples, "Have them sit down in groups of [about] fifty." They did so and made them all sit down. Then taking the five loaves and the two fish, and looking up to heaven, he said the blessing over them, broke them, and gave them to the disciples to set before the crowd. They all ate and were satisfied. And when the leftover fragments were picked up, they filled twelve wicker baskets.

## Luke 22:39-44

*His sweat became like drops of blood falling to the ground.*

THEN GOING OUT he went, as was his custom, to the Mount of Olives, and the disciples followed him. When he arrived at the place he said to them, "Pray that you may not undergo the test." After withdrawing about a stone's throw from them and kneeling, he prayed, saying, "Father, if you are willing, take this cup away from me; still, not my will but yours be done." [And to strengthen him an angel from heaven appeared to him. He was in such agony and he prayed so fervently that his sweat became like drops of blood falling on the ground.]

## Luke 24:13-35

*They recognized him at the breaking of the bread.*

NOW THAT VERY DAY two of them were going to a village seven miles from Jerusalem called Emmaus, and they were conversing about all the things that had occurred. And it happened that while they were conversing and debating, Jesus himself drew near and walked with them, but their eyes were prevented from recognizing him. He asked them, "What are you discussing as you walk along?" They stopped, looking downcast. One of them, named Cleopas, said to him in reply, "Are you the only visitor to Jerusalem who does not know of the things that have taken place there in these days?" And he replied to them, "What sort of things?" They said to him, "The things that happened to Jesus the Nazarene, who was a prophet mighty in deed and word before God and all the people, how our chief priests and rulers both handed him over to a sentence of death and crucified him. But we were hoping that he would be the one to redeem Israel; and besides all this, it is now the third day since this took place. Some women from our group, however, have astounded us: they were at the tomb early in the morning and did not find his body; they came back and reported that they had indeed seen a vision of angels who announced that he was alive. Then some of those with us went to the tomb and found things just as the women had described, but him they did not see." And he said to them, "Oh, how foolish you are! How slow of heart to believe all that the prophets spoke! Was it not necessary that the Messiah should suffer these things and enter into his glory?" Then beginning with Moses and all the prophets, he interpreted to them what referred to him in all the scriptures. As they approached the village to which they were going, he gave the impression that he was going on farther. But they urged him, "Stay with us, for it is nearly evening and the day is almost over." So he went in to stay with them. And it happened that, while he was with them at table, he took bread, said the blessing, broke it, and gave it to them. With that their eyes were opened and they recognized him, but he vanished from their sight. Then they said to each other, "Were not our hearts burning [within us] while he spoke to us on the way and opened the scriptures to us?" So they set out at once and returned to Jerusalem where they found gathered together the eleven and those with them who were saying, "The Lord has truly been raised and has appeared to Simon!" Then the two recounted what had taken place on the way and how he was made known to them in the breaking of the bread.

~ ❄ ~

## John 6:1-15

*They gave the people all the food they wanted.*

AFTER THIS, Jesus went across the Sea of Galilee [of Tiberias]. A large crowd followed him, because they saw the signs he was performing on the sick. Jesus went up on the mountain, and there he sat down with his disciples. The Jewish feast of Passover was near. When Jesus raised his eyes and saw that a large crowd was coming to him, he said to Philip, "Where can we buy enough food for them to eat?" He said this to test him, because he himself knew what he was going to do. Philip answered him, "Two hundred days' wages worth of food would not be enough for each of them to have a little [bit]." One of his disciples, Andrew, the brother of Simon Peter, said to him, "There is a boy here who has five barley loaves and two fish; but what good are these for so many?" Jesus said, "Have the people recline." Now there was a great deal of grass in that place. So the men reclined, about five thousand in number. Then Jesus took the loaves, gave thanks, and distributed them to those who were reclining, and also as much of the fish as they wanted. When they had had their fill, he said to his disciples, "Gather the fragments left over, so that nothing will be wasted." So they collected them, and filled twelve wicker baskets with fragments from the five barley loaves that had been more than they could eat. When the people saw the sign he had done, they said, "This is truly the Prophet, the one who is to come into the world." Since Jesus knew that they were going to come and cGarry him off to make him king, he withdrew again to the mountain alone.

~ ❈ ~

## John 6:24-35

*If you come to me, you will never be hungry.*
*He who believes in me will never know thirst.*

WHEN THE CROWD saw that neither Jesus nor his disciples were there, they themselves got into boats and came to Capernaum looking for Jesus. And when they found him across the sea they said to him, "Rabbi, when did you get here?" Jesus answered them and said, "Amen, amen, I say to you, you are looking for me not because you saw signs but because you ate the loaves and were filled. Do not work for food that perishes but for the food that endures for eternal life, which the Son of Man will give you. For on him the Father, God, has set his seal." So they said to him, "What can we do to accomplish the works of God?" Jesus answered and said to them, "This is the work of God, that you believe in the one he sent." So they said to him, "What sign can you do, that we may see and believe in you? What can you do? Our ancestors ate manna in the desert, as it is written: 'He gave them bread from heaven to eat.'"

So Jesus said to them, "Amen, amen, I say to you, it was not Moses who gave the bread from heaven; my Father gives you the true bread from heaven. For the bread of God is that which comes down from heaven and gives life to the world."

So they said to him, "Sir, give us this bread always." Jesus said to them, "I am the bread of life; whoever comes to me will never hunger, and whoever believes in me will never thirst."

～ ❋ ～

## John 6:41-51

*I am the living bread from heaven.*

THE JEWS murmured about him because he said, "I am the bread that came down from heaven," and they said, "Is this not Jesus, the son of Joseph? Do we not know his father and mother? Then how can he say, 'I have come down from heaven'?" Jesus answered and said to them, "Stop murmuring among yourselves. No one can come to me unless the Father who sent me draw him, and I will raise him on the last day. It is written in the prophets:

'They shall all be taught by God.'
Everyone who listens to my Father and learns from him comes to me. Not that anyone has seen the Father except the one who is from God; he has seen the Father. Amen, amen, I say to you, whoever believes has eternal life. I am the bread of life. Your ancestors ate the manna in the desert, but they died; this is the bread that comes down from heaven so that one may eat it and not die. I am the living bread that came down from heaven; whoever eats this bread will live forever; and the bread that I will give is my flesh for the life of the world."

## John 6:51-58

*My flesh and blood are true food and drink.*

"I AM the living bread that came down from heaven; whoever eats this bread will live forever; and the bread that I will give is my flesh for the life of the world."

The Jews quarreled among themselves, saying, "How can this man give us [his] flesh to eat?" Jesus said to them, "Amen, amen, I say to you, unless you eat the flesh of the Son of Man and drink his blood, you do not have life within you. Whoever eats my flesh and drinks my blood has eternal life, and I will raise him on the last day. For my flesh is true food, and my blood is true drink. Whoever eats my flesh and drinks my blood remains in me and I in him. Just as the living Father sent me and I have life because of the Father, so also the one who feeds on me will have life because of me. This is the bread that came down from heaven. Unlike your ancestors who ate and still died, whoever eats this bread will live forever."

## John 14:1-6

*I am the way and the truth and the life.*

JESUS said to his disciples: "Do not let your hearts be troubled. You have faith in God; have faith also in me. In my Father's house there are many dwelling places. If there were not, would I have told you that I am going to prepare a place for you? And if I go and prepare a place for you, I will come back again and take you to myself, so that where I am you also may be. Where I am going you know the way." Thomas said to him, "Master, we do not know where you are going; how can we know the way?" Jesus said to him, "I am the way and the truth and the life. No one comes to the Father except through me."

～ ❖ ～

## John 21:1-14

*Jesus took the bread and gave it to them.*

AFTER THIS, Jesus revealed himself again to his disciples at the Sea of Tiberias. He revealed himself in this way. Together were Simon Peter, Thomas called Didymus, Nathanael from Cana in Galilee, Zebedee's sons, and two others of his disciples. Simon Peter said to them, "I am going fishing." They said to him, "We also will come with you." So they went out and got into the boat, but that night they caught nothing. When it was already dawn, Jesus was standing on the shore; but the disciples did not realize that it was Jesus. Jesus said to them, "Children, have you caught anything to eat?" They answered him, "No." So he said to them, "Cast the net over the right side of the boat and you will find something." So they cast it, and were not able to pull it in because of the number of fish. So the disciple whom Jesus loved said to Peter, "It is the Lord." When Simon Peter heard that it was the Lord, he tucked in his garment, for he was lightly clad, and jumped into the sea. The other disciples came in the boat, for they were not far from shore, only about a hundred yards, dragging the net with the fish. When they climbed out on shore, they saw a charcoal fire with fish on it and bread. Jesus said to them, "Bring some of the fish you just caught." So Simon Peter went over and dragged the net ashore full of one hundred fifty-three large fish. Even though there were so many, the net was not torn. Jesus said to them, "Come, have breakfast." And none of the disciples dared to ask him, "Who are you?" because they realized it was the Lord. Jesus came over and took the bread and gave it to them, and in like manner the fish. This was now the third time Jesus was revealed to his disciples after being raised from the dead.

# OTHER NEW TESTAMENT SCRIPTURE PASSAGES

## Acts 2:42-47

*They continued in fellowship with the apostles and in the breaking of the bread.*

THEY DEVOTED THEMSELVES to the teaching of the apostles and to the communal life, to the breaking of the bread and to the prayers. Awe came upon everyone, and many wonders and signs were done through the apostles. All who believed were together and had all things in common; they would sell their property and possessions and divide them among all according to each one's need. Every day they devoted themselves to meeting together in the temple area and to breaking bread in their homes. They ate their meals with exultation and sincerity of heart, praising God and enjoying favor with all the people. And every day the Lord added to their number those who were being saved.

## Acts 10:34a, 36-43

*After he was raised from the dead, we ate and drank with him.*

THEN PETER proceeded to speak and said, "You know…what has happened all over Judea, beginning in Galilee after the baptism that John preached, how God anointed Jesus of Nazareth with the holy Spirit and power. He went about doing good and healing all those oppressed by the devil, for God was with him.

We are witnesses of all that he did both in the country of the Jews and [in] Jerusalem. They put him to death by hanging him on a tree. This man God raised [on] the third day and granted that he be visible, not to all the people, but to us, the witnesses chosen by God in advance, who ate and drank with him after he rose from the dead. He commissioned us to preach to the people and testify that he is the one appointed by God as judge of the living and the dead. To him all the prophets bear witness, that everyone who believes in him will receive forgiveness of sins through his name."

## 1 Corinthians 10:16-17

*Though we are many, we are one bread and one body.*

THE CUP OF BLESSING that we bless, is it not a participation in the blood of Christ? The bread that we break, is it not a participation in the body of Christ? Because the loaf of bread is one, we, though many, are one body, for we all partake of the one loaf.

## 1 Corinthians 11:23-26

*Each time you eat this bread and drink this cup, you are proclaiming the death of the Lord Jesus.*

FOR I RECEIVED from the Lord what I also handed on to you, that the Lord Jesus, on the night he was handed over, took bread, and, after he had given thanks, broke it and said, "This is my body that is for you. Do this in remembrance of me." In the same way also the cup, after supper, saying, "This cup is the new covenant in my blood. Do this, as often as you drink it, in remembrance of me." For as often as you eat this bread and drink the cup, you proclaim the death of the Lord until he comes.

## Hebrews 9:11-15

*The blood of Christ purifies our hearts from sin.*

**B**UT WHEN CHRIST came as high priest of the good things that have come to be, passing through the greater and more perfect tabernacle not made by hands, that is, not belonging to this creation, he entered once for all into the sanctuary, not with the blood of goats and calves but with his own blood, thus obtaining eternal redemption. For if the blood of goats and bulls and the sprinkling of a heifer's ashes can sanctify those who are defiled so that their flesh is cleansed, how much more will the blood of Christ, who through the eternal spirit offered himself unblemished to God, cleanse our consciences from dead works to worship the living God.

For this reason he is mediator of a new covenant: since a death has taken place for deliverance from transgressions under the first covenant, those who are called may receive the promised eternal inheritance.

## Hebrews 12:18-19, 22-24

*Jesus brings you to the Father by shedding his blood for you.*

YOU HAVE not approached that which could be touched and a blazing fire and gloomy darkness and storm and a trumpet blast and a voice speaking words such that those who heard begged that no message be further addressed to them. No, you have approached Mount Zion and the city of the living God, the heavenly Jerusalem, and countless angels in festal gathering, and the assembly of the firstborn enrolled in heaven, and God the judge of all, and the spirits of the just made perfect, and Jesus, the mediator of a new covenant, and the sprinkled blood that speaks more eloquently than that of Abel.

## 1 Peter 1:17-21

*You have been redeemed by the precious blood of Christ.*

NOW if you invoke as Father him who judges impartially according to each one's works, conduct yourselves with reverence during the time of your sojourning, realizing that you were ransomed from your futile conduct, handed on by your ancestors, not with perishable things like silver or gold but with the precious blood of Christ as of a spotless unblemished lamb. He was known before the foundation of the world but revealed in the final time for you, who through him believe in God who raised him from the dead and gave him glory, so that your faith and hope are in God.

## 1 John 4:4-8

*The Spirit, the water, and the blood
give witness.*

You BELONG TO GOD, children, and you have conquered them, for the one who is in you is greater than the one who is in the world. They belong to the world; accordingly, their teaching belongs to the world, and the world listens to them. We belong to God, and anyone who knows God listens to us, while anyone who does not belong to God refuses to hear us. This is how we know the spirit of truth and the spirit of deceit.

Beloved, let us love one another, because love is of God; everyone who loves is begotten by God and knows God. Whoever is without love does not know God, for God is love.

## Revelation 1:4-8

*Because he loves us, he has saved us from sin
with his blood.*

Grace TO YOU and peace... from Jesus Christ, the faithful witness, the firstborn of the dead and ruler of the kings of the earth. To him who loves us and has freed us from our sins by his blood, who has made us into a kingdom, priests for his God and Father, to him be glory and power forever [and ever]. Amen.

Behold, he is coming amid the clouds,
   and every eye will see him,
   even those who pierced him.
All the peoples of the earth will lament him.
   Yes. Amen.

"I am the Alpha and the Omega," says the Lord God, "the one who is and who was and who is to come, the almighty."

## Revelation 7:9-14

*They have washed their robes in the blood of the Lamb.*

AFTER THIS I had a vision of a great multitude, which no one could count, from every nation, race, people, and tongue. They stood before the throne and before the Lamb, wearing white robes and holding palm branches in their hands. They cried out in a loud voice:

"Salvation comes from our God, who is seated on the throne, and from the Lamb."

All the angels stood around the throne and around the elders and the four living creatures. They prostrated themselves before the throne, worshiped God, and exclaimed:

"Amen. Blessing and glory, wisdom and thanksgiving, honor, power, and might
be to our God forever and ever. Amen."

Then one of the elders spoke up and said to me, "Who are these wearing white robes, and where did they come from?" I said to him, "My lord, you are the one who knows." He said to me, "These are the ones who have survived the time of great distress; they have washed their robes and made them white in the blood of the Lamb."

# OLD TESTAMENT
# SCRIPTURE PASSAGES

## Genesis 14:18-20

*Melchizedek brought bread and wine.*

MELCHIZEDEK, king of Salem, brought out bread and wine. He was a priest of God Most High. He blessed Abram with these words:
"Blessed be Abram by God Most High,
   the creator of heaven and earth;
And blessed be God Most High,
   who delivered your foes into your hand."
Then Abram gave him a tenth of everything.

## Exodus 12:21-27

*When the Lord sees the blood on the door,*
*he will pass over your home.*

MOSES summoned all the elders of Israel and said to them, "Go and procure lambs for your families, and slaughter the Passover victims. Then take a bunch of hyssop, and dipping it in the blood that is in the basin, apply some of this blood to the lintel and the two doorposts. And none of you shall go outdoors until morning. For when the LORD goes by to strike down the Egyptians, seeing the blood on the lintel and the two doorposts, the LORD will pass over that door and not let the destroyer come into your houses to strike you down.

"You will keep this practice forever as a statute for yourselves and your descendants. Thus, when you have entered the land which the LORD will give you as he promised, you must observe this rite. When your children ask you, 'What does this rite of yours mean?' you will reply, 'It is the Passover sacrifice for the LORD, who passed over the houses of the Israelites in Egypt; when he struck down the Egyptians, he delivered our houses.'"

## Exodus 16:2-4, 12-15

*I will rain bread from heaven upon you.*

HERE IN THE WILDERNESS the whole Israelite community grumbled against Moses and Aaron. The Israelites said to them, "If only we had died at the LORD's hand in the land of Egypt, as we sat by our kettles of meat and ate our fill of bread! But you have led us into this wilderness to make this whole assembly die of famine!"

Then the LORD said to Moses: I am going to rain down bread from heaven for you. Each day the people are to go out and gather their daily portion; thus will I test them, to see whether they follow my instructions or not.

I have heard the grumbling of the Israelites. Tell them: In the evening twilight you will eat meat, and in the morning you will have your fill of bread, and then you will know that I, the LORD, am your God.

In the evening, quail came up and covered the camp. In the morning there was a layer of dew all about the camp, and when the layer of dew evaporated, fine flakes were on the surface of the wilderness, fine flakes like hoarfrost on the ground. On seeing it, the Israelites asked one another, "What is this?" for they did not know what it was. But Moses told them, "It is the bread which the LORD has given you to eat."

## Exodus 24:3-8

*This is the blood of the covenant that the Lord God has made with you.*

WHEN MOSES CAME to the people and related all the words and ordinances of the LORD, they all answered with one voice, "We will do everything that the LORD has told us." Moses then wrote down all the words of the LORD and, rising early in the morning, he built at the foot of the mountain an altar and twelve sacred stones for the twelve tribes of Israel. Then, having sent young men of the Israelites to offer burnt offerings and sacrifice young bulls as communion offerings to the LORD, Moses took half of the blood and put it in large bowls; the other half he splashed on the altar. Taking the book of the covenant, he read it aloud to the people, who answered, "All that the LORD has said, we will hear and do." Then he took the blood and splashed it on the people, saying, "This is the blood of the covenant which the LORD has made with you according to all these words."

## Deuteronomy 8:2-3

*He gave you food which you and your fathers did not know.*

REMEMBER HOW for these forty years the LORD, your God, has directed all your journeying in the wilderness, so as to test you by affliction, to know what was in your heart:

to keep his commandments, or not. He therefore let you be afflicted with hunger, and then fed you with manna, a food unknown to you and your ancestors, so you might know that it is not by bread alone that people live, but by all that comes forth from the mouth of the LORD.

## 1 Kings 19:4-8

*Strengthened by the food, he walked to the mountain of the Lord.*

[H]E] WENT a day's journey into the wilderness, until he came to a solitary broom tree and sat beneath it. He prayed for death: "Enough, LORD! Take my life, for I am no better than my ancestors." He lay down and fell asleep under the solitary broom tree, but suddenly a messenger touched him and said, "Get up and eat!" He looked and there at his head was a hearth cake and a jug of water. After he ate and drank, he lay down again, but the angel of the LORD came back a second time, touched him, and said, "Get up and eat or the journey will be too much for you!" He got up, ate, and drank; then strengthened by that food, he walked forty days and forty nights to the mountain of God, Horeb.

## Proverbs 9:1-6

*Come and eat my bread, drink the wine I have prepared.*

WISDOM has built her house, she has set up her seven columns; She has prepared her meat, mixed her wine, yes, she has spread her table.

She has sent out her maidservants; she calls
>from the heights out over the city:
"Let whoever is naive turn in here;
>to any who lack sense I say,
Come, eat of my food,
>and drink of the wine I have mixed!
Forsake foolishness that you may live;
>advance in the way of understanding."

# PSALMS

## PSALM 63

O God, you are my God—
it is you I seek!
For you my body yearns;
for you my soul thirsts,
In a land parched, lifeless,
and without water.
I look to you in the sanctuary
to see your power and glory.

For your love is better than life;
my lips shall ever praise you!
I will bless you as long as I live;
I will lift up my hands, calling on your name.
My soul shall be sated as with choice food,
with joyous lips my mouth shall praise you!

I think of you upon my bed,
I remember you through the watches of the night
You indeed are my savior,
and in the shadow of your wings I shout for joy.
My soul clings fast to you;
your right hand upholds me.

But those who seek my life will come to ruin;
they shall go down
    to the depths of the netherworld!
Those who would hand over my life
    to the sword shall
become the prey of jackals!

But the king shall rejoice in God;
all who swear by the Lord shall exult,
but the mouths of liars will be shut!

## PSALM 110

The LORD says to my lord:
"Sit at my right hand,
while I make your enemies your footstool."

The scepter of your might:
the LORD extends your strong scepter from Zion.
Have dominion over your enemies!

Yours is princely power
from the day of your birth.

In holy splendor before the daystar,
like dew I begot you.

The LORD has sworn and will not waver:
"You are a priest forever
in the manner of Melchizedek."

At your right hand is the Lord,
who crushes kings on the day of his wrath,

Who judges nations, heaps up corpses,
crushes heads across the wide earth,

Who drinks from the brook by the wayside
and thus holds high his head.

*Psalm 111*

Hallelujah!

I will praise the Lord with all my heart
in the assembled congregation of the upright.
Great are the works of the Lord,
studied by all who delight in them.

Majestic and glorious is his work,
his righteousness endures forever.
He won renown for his wondrous deeds;
gracious and merciful is the Lord.

He gives food to those who fear him,
he remembers his covenant forever.
He showed his powerful deeds to his people,
giving them the inheritance of the nations.

The works of his hands are true and just,
reliable all his decrees,
Established forever and ever,
to be observed with truth and equity.

He sent release to his people,
decreed his covenant forever;
holy and fearsome is his name.

The fear of the Lord is the beginning of wisdom;
prudent are all who practice it.
His praise endures forever.

~ ✤ ~

## Psalm 116 [10-19]

I kept faith, even when I said,
"I am greatly afflicted!"
I said in my alarm,
"All men are liars!"

How can I repay the LORD
for all the great good done for me?
I will raise the cup of salvation
and call on the name of the LORD.

I will pay my vows to the LORD
in the presence of all his people.
Dear in the eyes of the LORD
is the death of his devoted.

LORD, I am your servant,
your servant, the child of your maidservant;
you have loosed my bonds.
I will offer a sacrifice of praise
and call on the name of the LORD.

I will pay my vows to the LORD
in the presence of all his people,
In the courts of the house of the LORD,
in your midst, O Jerusalem.

Hallelujah!

～ ✤ ～

# Saints Who Loved the Eucharist

## by Lisa Lickona

# Saints Who Loved the Eucharist

*Let the children come to me, and do not prevent them; for the kingdom of heaven belongs to such as these* (Mt 19:14). These words of Christ seem to be a call from the tabernacle—for so many of the saints who exhibited an intense love for our Eucharistic Lord were drawn to him as children. Little Peter Julian Eymard stole into the church to rest his head on the altar. Geltrude Comensoli hid herself in her mother's shawl and sneaked early to the Communion rail. The altar boy Tarcisius suffered death rather than relinquish the Holy Body. And, to these "official" saints, we might add the unnamed Chinese girl who went to a desecrated church each night for a month to consume the hosts that were spilled there. On the last night she was caught and killed by the Boxer rebels. This child inspired the Eucharistic devotion of Venerable Fulton Sheen, who declared, "*The greatest love story of all time is contained in a tiny white Host.*"

Every spring, in parishes all over the country, seven-year-olds receive our Lord for the first time—the boys uncharacteristically serious, the girls arrayed in white. Let us preserve that same joy and expectation all our lives, letting our hearts be drawn to him whose yoke is easy and whose burden is light.

*Lord of all, draw me to the altar where
I receive the food for my journey, the blessed
and broken Body of your Son.*

# Saint Peter Julian Eymard

Founder († 1868)                                    Feast: August 2

Peter was born in La Mure d'Isère, France. Before his birth, his mother had borne three children who had died in infancy. But Peter flourished, and his mother often took him in her arms when she went to pray in gratitude before the Blessed Sacrament. When Peter was five, he disappeared one day. His stepsister discovered him in the church. He was standing at the top of a ladder that he had found and leaned against the high altar. "I can listen better to Jesus from here," he told his sister.

Eventually Peter entered the seminary and was ordained. Five years later he received permission to join the Marist order. But after a few years another desire took hold of him, planted in his heart on the feast of Corpus Christi, 1845: "to bring all the world to the knowledge and love of our Lord; to preach nothing but Jesus Christ, and Jesus Christ Eucharistic."

Despite the many difficulties, Peter left one order to found another: the Congregation of the Blessed Sacrament. Eventually, an order of nuns followed and then lay and priestly associations—all centered on the Blessed Sacrament. The final years of Peter's life were filled with physical suffering, financial troubles, and continuous resistance to his work. Yet one friend, Saint John Vianney, said, "Adoration by priests! How wonderful!... I will pray for his work every day."

*My Lord in heaven, through the intercession of Saint Peter Julian Eymard, ignite within my heart a fervent love for your Eucharistic presence.*

# Saint Geltrude Comensoli

Foundress († 1903)                               Feast: February 18

From her earliest years, little Caterina found solace in prayer. When her playmates asked what she was doing, looking so serious, she would say, "I am thinking." At seven, she donned her mother's thick black shawl and presented herself at the Communion rail. This secret First Communion was a source of hidden strength.

At fifteen, Caterina entered religious life, but illness drove her home. She took a job as a domestic servant and made a private vow of chastity. She taught poor girls. And, with her spiritual director, Father Spinelli, she began to plan a congregation of women devoted to adoration of the Blessed Sacrament. A meeting with Pope Leo XIII arranged by her employer ended with the pope encouraging Caterina to have her sisters extend Jesus' presence among the poor workers, in whose lives little time remained for silent prayer. In 1882, the Sacramentine Sisters were born, and Caterina became Sister Geltrude of the Blessed Sacrament.

"Jesus Christ lives in our midst to be close and ready to help us always," Geltrude said. "Love keeps him a prisoner in a Host, hidden night and day in the holy tabernacle. He has his delight in the inaccessible light of the Father and yet delights to be with men." Since her death in 1903, her sisters have grown to ninety communities on three continents.

*Lord Jesus, through the intercession of Saint Geltrude Comensoli, grant me childlike impetuousness, that I might come to you without resistance!*

# Saint Michael de Sanctis

Priest († 1625)                                               Feast: April 10

Michael Argemir was born in Vich, Catalonia, Spain, in 1591. As a child he longed to imitate Saint Francis' pursuit of holy poverty, but, after the death of his parents, he was educated for the mercantile trade. Yet young Michael was quite determined. At the age of twelve he made his way to the door of the Trinitarians in Barcelona and begged entry. At fifteen he made his vows in Saragossa. Soon after, he moved to the discalced Trinitarians at Madrid, attracted by their austere life and the depth of prayer it made possible. Among them he became Michael de Sanctis, Michael "of the Saints."

Michael was ordained and became superior of the house at Valladolid. He preached in the neighboring towns and helped the poor and the needy at every opportunity. Long hours spent in prayer before the Blessed Sacrament sustained him. When he said Mass, he was swept into a state of rapture at the moment of the consecration. Among the Trinitarians he became known as "the ecstatic one."

Michael died in Vallodolid on April 10, 1625, at the age of thirty-three. Artistic depictions of Michael show him kneeling before a monstrance, clothed in his Trinitarian habit, with its characteristic red and blue crosses. He was canonized in 1862 and is especially invoked by those suffering from cancer.

*Lord Jesus, through the intercession of Saint Michael de Sanctis, shield me from worldly anxiety. Grant me inner calm each time I kneel before your altar.*

# Saint Tarcisius

Acolyte († 3rd century)                                    Feast: August 15

We learn of Tarcisius in a poem by Saint Damasus, who tells us that he "suffered death rather than surrender the Sacred Body to the dogs." The story, as retold in our time by Pope Benedict XVI in his Wednesday Audience of August 4, 2010, is that Tarcisius was an acolyte, or altar server—a secret Christian under the Roman emperor Valerian. After serving Mass one day, he volunteered to take the Eucharist to the sick and imprisoned, despite the great risks involved. "My youth," Tarcisius declared, "will be the best shield for the Eucharist."

Tarcisius secured the sacred hosts in a linen bag that he placed close to his heart. As he went along, he met some other boys, who wondered what he was clutching so earnestly. When Tarcisius resisted their questioning, they became more insistent. Tarcisius, they suddenly realized, must be one of the Christians. The boys began to struggle with Tarcisius; blows fell and rocks were thrown. By the time Quadratus, a Christian member of the Praetorian guard, stepped in, Tarcisius was already dying.

The young boy was carried to the catacombs of Saint Callistus. The host that he had been guarding so fiercely was found to have become one with his own flesh, "thereby forming, together with his body, a single immaculate Host offered to God."

*Lord Jesus, through the intercession of Saint Tarcisius, whenever I am attacked and maligned, then draw me closer to you.*

# Saint Francis Carraciolo

Founder († 1608)                                           Feast: June 4

Francis was born Ascanio, the son of an Italian nobleman, a distant relative of Saint Thomas Aquinas. In his twenties, he was struck with a serious skin disease presumed by others to be leprosy. He begged God for healing, promising that he would devote his life to the Gospel. When the disease cleared suddenly, Ascanio went to Naples to minister to prisoners.

A letter gone astray gave him his life's work. John Augustine Adorno of Genoa had written to another Ascanio Carraciolo to ask his help in founding an order of priests devoted to both prayer and pastoral work. The missive accidentally came to our Ascanio, who saw in it the hand of God. He went to meet Adorno and together they founded the Minor Clerks Regular, in 1588. Ascanio took the name Francis. The two men created a rule for those who joined them: regular penances, a vow to refuse appointed office, and—most important for Francis—perpetual adoration of the Blessed Sacrament. Houses were founded at Naples and in Spain.

When Francis was named superior, he led all in pastoral work—hearing confessions, begging for the poor, preaching Christ to all. Although ill health forced him to resign at the age of forty-four, he continued to live austerely, making a home under the stairs of a house in Naples. He died at Agnone on the vigil of Corpus Christi.

*Lord Jesus, through the intercession of Saint Francis Carraciolo, help me to see your loving care behind all that happens to me—even the accidents that befall me.*

# Saint Maria Cristina Brando

Foundress (✝ 1906)                    Feast: January 20

Maria Cristina was born Adelaide Brando, of wealthy parents in Naples, Italy. Her mother died soon after she was born. Little Adelaide grew to be a child of unusual sensitivity; above all, she felt deeply for Christ Crucified. "I must become holy; I want to be a saint," she was heard to say. At twelve she made a vow of perpetual virginity.

After some years, Adelaide entered the novitiate of the Poor Clares, becoming Maria Cristina. But illness intervened, and she was sent home. After her recovery, she entered the Sacramentine sisters, but sickness again forced her to leave. So she formed a new plan: to found an order of sisters devoted to prayers of reparation before the Blessed Sacrament and the care of children and the most vulnerable. With the help of her friends Saint Ludovico of Casoria and Venerable Michelangelo of Marigliano, she laid the groundwork for the order. In 1884, she and some other young women moved to a house in Casoria. A shrine to the Blessed Sacrament was constructed; Maria Cristina dwelt in a cell nearby, the groticella or "little grotto." She spent her nights keeping watch with her Eucharistic Lord.

The Sisters Expiatory Victims of Jesus in the Blessed Sacrament were formally recognized in 1903, three years before Maria Cristina's death. She was canonized by Pope Francis on October 20, 2014.

*My Lord and Savior, through the intercession of Saint Maria Cristina Brando, make my heart a place where your love might abide.*

# Saint Stanisław Sołtys Kazimierczyk

Founder († 1489)                                    Feast: May 3

Stanisław was baptized Louis, the son of wealthy, devout parents in Kazimierz, now a part of Kraków, Poland. He was educated by the Canons Regular of the Lateran at the school attached to the Church of Corpus Christi. Louis went on to study theology and philosophy at Jagiellonian University. At the age of twenty-three, he returned to his hometown to join the Canons, taking the name Stanisław, after the saintly bishop who was martyred close to his home.

After ordination, Stanisław rose quickly to positions of leadership, first vice prior and then novice master. He spent himself in the care of the needy and the destitute of the neighborhood, and many hearts were healed in his confessional. Stanisław preached passionately against the heretical doctrines concerning the Eucharist then being circulated by followers of the Czech priest Jan Hus. His vigilant defense of the doctrine of the Real Presence earned him the title "Apostle of the Blessed Sacrament."

After Stanisław's death in 1489, a devotion grew up among the people of Kraków. The official cause for the priest who had been known for centuries as "blessed" was finally introduced in the 20th century by then-Archbishop Karol Wojtyła. As Pope John Paul II, he presided over Stanisław's beatification. Pope Benedict pronounced Stanisław a saint in 2010: "His whole life was bound to the Eucharist."

*Merciful Lord, through the intercession of Saint Stanisław Sołtys Kazimierczyk, make me a servant of my neighbors.*

# Saint Thomas Aquinas

Priest and Doctor of the Church († 1274)          Feast: January 28

An Italian nobleman, Thomas joined the Dominican friars in Naples around the year 1244, only to be promptly kidnapped by his brothers. Thomas was willing to wait them out, and spent his imprisonment in study. Once freed, he went to study theology at the University of Paris under Saint Albert the Great. After receiving his doctorate, he taught, preached, and wrote with intense energy. His magnum opus, the *Summa Theologiae*, remains an unparalleled synthesis of the Church's theology.

At the command of Pope Urban IV, Thomas penned the liturgy for the feast of Corpus Christi, and from this we draw the Benediction hymns *"Tantum Ergo"* and *"O Salutaris Hostia."* Another Eucharistic hymn, *"Adoro Te Devote,"* was originally a personal prayer written by Thomas when he attended his second Mass of the day, not as celebrant but as participant. The moving poetry of this hymn has inspired over sixteen English translations.

In 1273, moved by an intense experience he had while saying Mass, Thomas left off writing. The next year, he fell gravely ill while en route to the Second Council of Lyons. He was brought Viaticum on his deathbed. "I receive thee, ransom of my soul," he declared. "For love of thee have I studied and kept vigil, toiled, preached, and taught...."

*My Jesus, my all, through the intercession of Saint Thomas Aquinas, grant me silence and space that I might contemplate your wondrous love.*

# Saint Peter of Alcántara

Founder († 1562)    Feast: October 19

A native of Alcántara in the province of Estremadura, Spain, Peter experienced a call to the Franciscans at the age of fifteen. By twenty-two, he had been charged with founding a new Franciscan house at Badajoz. Seeing the many ills besetting his brethren, Peter's prescription was reform. He lived the poverty he advocated, owning only one tunic, and eating but once every three days.

Not all of Peter's fellow Franciscans embraced his reforms, and, for a time, he retired to live as a hermit at Arabida. Other like-minded friars found him there and began to follow his ways. In 1554, Peter received official recognition of his reformed branch of the Franciscans.

Like his spiritual father, Saint Francis, Peter's attachment to our Lord was expressed in his preaching and his prayer. On the Eucharist, Peter taught, "No tongue can express the greatness of the love which Jesus Christ bears to our souls. He did not wish that between him and his servants there should be any other pledge than himself, to keep alive the remembrance of him." Peter's intense experience of being loved by Jesus was manifested in prayers of ecstasy. His friend and fellow reformer Saint Teresa of Ávila once witnessed one of these transports of love. Peter died in Estremadura in 1562.

*My Jesus, through the intercession of Saint Peter of Alcántara, help me to know your tender love expressed in your Body and Blood, given for us.*

# Saint Euphrasia Eluvathingal

Virgin († 1952)                                    Feast: August 29

Euphrasia received the name Rose at her birth in the village of Katoor, in the Syro-Malabar Catholic archdiocese of Trichur, Kerala, India. Her mother taught her about her namesake, the mystic and penitent Rose of Lima. When Rose was seven, the Blessed Mother came to her and taught her to pray with the angels. After she began her education with the Carmelite sisters, she expressed the desire to follow them. Her father fiercely resisted the idea. He was finally won over, in part by Rose's intense prayer and daily self-sacrifice.

In 1897, Rose entered the Congregation of the Mother of Carmel. As Euphrasia of the Sacred Heart of Jesus, she professed her vows on May 24, 1900. Her frail health was belied by her joyful affection for Jesus who had come to her and asked her to be his spouse. She spent many hours before the Blessed Sacrament each day. When she left the convent chapel, it seemed that the Lord's presence moved with her. The sisters called her the "moving Tabernacle" or, simply, "the praying Mother."

Euphrasia prayed for the sick persons the sisters served—especially those suffering from cholera and tuberculosis. She took on penances for the pope, bishops, priests, and religious. After her death in 1952, many of those who had benefitted from her prayer testified to her great generosity of soul.

*Dear Jesus, through the intercession of Saint Euphrasia Eluvathingal, make me one who bears your love to the broken ones.*

# Saint Peter Chrysologus

Bishop and Doctor of the Church († c. 450)  Feast: July 30

What little we know of Peter's life comes from his own writings and a 9th-century biography. He was born in Imola, Italy. Cornelius, the bishop of Imola, educated him and ordained him deacon. Around the year 425, Peter was named Archbishop of Ravenna.

Later generations surnamed Peter *Chrysologus* or "golden-worded." He authored a number of theological treatises, only one of which, a letter to the heretic Eutyches, has come down to us. What we do have are Peter's sermons, 176 in all, packed with his insight into the Scriptures. A modern commentator has remarked that few of Peter's sermons would have required more than five minutes to deliver, making them a marvel of brevity in the ancient world. In them, Peter consistently witnesses to the traditional belief in the Real Presence of Jesus in the Eucharist. "He is the Bread sown in the Virgin, leavened in the flesh, molded in his Passion, baked in the furnace of the sepulcher, placed in the churches, and set upon the altars, which daily supplies heavenly food to the faithful," Peter writes.

From the time of Peter's first sermon, the Empress Galla Placidia was moved to support generously his building efforts in Ravenna. Today the city remains as one of the jewels of Christendom. Peter is believed to have died at Imola around the year 450. He was named a Doctor of the Church in 1729.

*Word of God, through the intercession of Saint Peter Chrysologus, grant me wisdom and clarity when I speak of you.*

# Saint Paschasius Radbertus

Abbot († 865) Feast: April 26

Paschasius Radbertus was a foundling child. The nuns of Notre-Dame at Soissons, France, took care of him as an infant and then sent him to the monastery of Saint Peter for his studies. He became a monk at Corbie near Amiens. Eventually he was elected abbot at Corbie, but, after seven years, he resigned and devoted his remaining years to study.

Paschasius mostly wrote learned commentaries on the Scriptures. But, in 831, he composed a short volume for his brother monks in Saxony, entitled *De Corpore et Sanguine Domini*, "On the Body and Blood of the Lord." In it he taught that, in the moment of consecration, the bread and wine are really changed into the Body and Blood of Jesus Christ such that there is "nothing else in the Eucharist but the flesh and blood of Christ," although "the figure of bread and wine remain."

Scholars consider Paschasius' treatise to be the first theological exposition of the doctrine of transubstantiation, although, perhaps inevitably, his formulations lacked some subtle distinctions. After he sent a revised copy of the treatise to Emperor Charles the Bald in 844, a controversy erupted among his fellow monks. This theological back-and-forth ultimately bore rich fruit in the full development of the Eucharistic doctrine some two centuries later.

*King of Eternal Glory, through the intercession of Saint Paschasius Radbertus, thank you for giving me your Eucharistic Body and Blood as my food, my drink, my true sustenance.*

# Saint Stanislaus Kostka

Religious († 1568)                         Feast: September 18

Stanislaus was born in 1550 in Rostkovo Castle. His father was a senator for the Polish kingdom and his mother a noblewoman. Stanislaus and his older brother Paul received a strict education before they were sent to the Jesuit college in Vienna in 1564. Already Stanislaus had exhibited a prodigious desire for prayer and penance. But Paul mocked him for his desire to become a religious.

Two years into his time at school, Stanislaus became dangerously ill. He asked to have Viaticum brought to him, but his landlord, a Lutheran, refused to let a priest enter the house. So Stanislaus had recourse to his patroness, Saint Barbara. He begged her to obtain the Sacrament for him. Stanislaus later told of how two angels appeared and brought him Communion. Mary came to him, too, and told him to enter the Jesuits.

After Stanislaus recovered from his sickness, he went to the Jesuits in Vienna, but they refused him for fear of his father's wrath. So Stanislaus left Vienna in secret and made for Rome, where he was received into the order. The new novice struck all those who met him; Saints Peter Canisius and Francis Borgia were both moved by his capacity for love. Only nine months into his novitiate, Stanislaus fell ill and died. He is the patron of those seeking Viaticum.

*Risen Lord, through the intercession of Saint Stanislaus Kostka, grant me absolute trust in your care for me now and at the hour of death.*

# Saint María Micaela Desmaisières

Foundress († 1865)                           Feast: August 24

María was born in Madrid in 1809. Her mother died when she was quite small. She lost her father at age thirteen. For four years María was educated among the Ursulines, and she developed a deep love for Jesus in the Blessed Sacrament. After school, she went to live with her brother, who served as a Spanish ambassador in Paris and Brussels. Life was a whirlwind of parties, balls, and concerts. In the midst of this busyness Maria remained quietly centered on Christ, spending many hours in Eucharistic adoration. Her daily Communion sustained her; her hidden penances kept her ever mindful of him.

At the age of thirty-five, María returned to Madrid and began to perform works of charity in the city. At the Hospital of Saint John of God, she met a "girl with a shawl," a "victim to an evil life." María's heart was moved. She founded and administered a school for desperate girls. Then, in 1856, she established the Congregation of the Handmaids of the Blessed Sacrament and Charity, to serve young women who had been drawn into prostitution.

After she was named Mother General in 1859, María redoubled her prayer, frequently spending entire nights in silent adoration. She became known as Madre Sacramento. She died in 1865 serving cholera victims in Valencia. Today her sisters continue to adore the Blessed Sacrament and help girls and women who have been exploited in human trafficking in Latin America and Asia.

*Father in heaven, through the intercession of Saint María Micaela, fire me with love for those who have been abused or abandoned.*

# Saint Paschal Baylon

Lay Brother († 1592)                                    Feast: May 17

Paschal was born of peasants in Torre Hermosa, the kingdom of Aragon, today part of Spain. He was named for the feast on which he was born, the "Pasch of the Holy Spirit," or Pentecost. From the age of seven, he spent long days herding sheep. His parents noticed that he had an unusual capacity for silent prayer. They saw how little Paschal taught the other shepherds, coarse men, to kneel down and give thanks. He loved to pray in the midst of his work when he heard the church bells ring for the consecration at Mass. And so, when he came to his parents and told them his plan to walk the 200 miles to the Loreto convent of the reformed Franciscans of Peter of Alcántara to become a lay brother, they did not refuse.

In the austere and devout atmosphere of the convent, Paschal flourished. He loved to serve the poor children who came to beg at the door. And he loved to spend long hours, sometimes entire nights, kneeling before the Eucharist, rapt in prayer. One day, one of the brothers came upon the locked refectory door and realized that Paschal had shut himself inside. Peering through the buttery hatch, the brother watched as Paschal performed a long dance in front of a statue of the Virgin. Such was Paschal's delight before his holy Mother!

Paschal died at Villareal at the age of fifty-two. Many miracles were reported at his grave. He was canonized in 1690, and, in 1897, Pope Leo XIII declared the humble lay brother the patron of all Eucharistic congresses and associations.

*Son of God and Son of Mary, through the intercession of Saint Paschal Baylon, grant me abundant joy in the presence of the Eucharist!*

# Acknowledgments

"What Is Adoration?"; "The Treasury of God's Mercy":
http://www.sacre-coeur-montmartre.com/english/
Reprinted by permission.

"Some word of counsel as you begin to adore" adapted from the popular French essay *"Dix conseils pratiques pour l'adoration du Saint Sacrement."*

Adoration in a Time of Need

First Hour Meditation from an unpublished manuscript.
Used with permission.

Second Hour Meditation taken from *Elisabeth Leseur: Selected Writings*, edited, translated, and introduced by Janet K. Ruffing, R.S.M.
© 2005, Janet K. Ruffing, Paulist Press, Inc., New York/Mahwah, NJ.
Reprinted by permission of Paulist Press, Inc. www.paulistpress.com

Third Hour Meditation "Ever in God's Hands" taken from General Audience on Wednesday, February 15, 2012. Published in L'Osservatore Romano, Weekly Edition in English, 22 February 2012, page 15.
Used with permission of the Libreria Editrice Vaticana. www.vatican.va

Magisterial Statements

*Sollemnis Professio Fidei* # 24, 25, 26
Used with permission of the Libreria Editrice Vaticana.
www.vatican.va

*Dominicae Cenae* # 3
Used with permission of the Libreria Editrice Vaticana.
www.vatican.va

Excerpts from the English translation of the Catechism of the Catholic Church for use in the United States of America © 1994, United States Catholic Conference, Inc.—Libreria Editrice Vaticana. Used with Permission. Modifications from the Editio Typica copyright © 1997, United States Conference of Catholic Bishops—Libreria Editrice Vaticana.

*Directory on Popular Piety and the Liturgy* # 164
Used with permission of the Libreria Editrice Vaticana.
www.vatican.va

*Ecclesia de Eucharistia* # 25
Used with permission of the Libreria Editrice Vaticana.
www.vatican.va

*Redemptionis Sacramentum* # 134, 135
Used with permission of the Libreria Editrice Vaticana.
www.vatican.va

*Sacramentum Caritatis* # 66, 67
Used with permission of the Libreria Editrice Vaticana.
www.vatican.va

*Lumen Fidei* # 31, 44. Used with permission of the Libreria Editrice Vaticana.
www.vatican.va


Meditations

**Pope Benedict XVI** - **"He is here, in our midst…"** taken from Apostolic
Journey of His Holiness Benedict XVI to France on the Occasion
of the 150th Anniversary of the Apparitions of the Blessed Virgin Mary
at Lourdes. September 12-15, 2008. Used with permission of the Libreria
Editrice Vaticana. www.vatican.va

**Saint Maria Faustina Kowalska** - **"Our Conversation, Our Secret"** taken
from *Diary of Saint Maria Faustina Kowalska, Divine Mercy in My Soul.*
Paragraph 1692. © 1987, Marian Press, Stockbridge, MA. Used with
permission of the Marian Fathers of the Immaculate Conception of the
B.V.M. www.faustina-message.com/diary-saint-sister-faustina.htm

**Saint John N. Neumann** - **"Consumed by the Fire of Love"** taken from
*Saint John N. Neumann's Favorite Prayers taken from His Diary.*
© Saint John Neumann Shrine, Philadelphia, PA. www.stjohnneumann.org.

**Saint Margaret Mary Alacoque** - **"A Life of Sacrifice"** taken from *The
Letters of Saint Margaret Mary Alacoque.* Father Clarence A. Herbst, s.j.,
Tr. © 1997 by TAN Books, Charlotte, NC (www.tanbooks.com).
Used with permission.

**Saint Thomas Aquinas** - **"O Marvelous Sacrament!"** taken from
*St. Thomas Aquinas, Selected Writings*, Rev. M.C. Darcy, Ed. Published
by Roman Catholic Books, Fort Collins, CO. www.BooksforCatholics.com.

**Blessed Charles de Foucauld** - **"In the Presence of the Beloved"** taken
from *Charles de Foucauld: Writings*, Robert Ellsberg, Ed. Copyright
© 1999, Orbis Books, Maryknoll, New York. www.orbisbooks.com.
Used with permission.

Saint John Bosco - "Bonds of Sublime Love" taken from *15 Days of Prayer with Don Bosco*, Robert Schiéle, Ed., Victoria Hébert and Denis Sabourin, Trs. © 2001, New City Press, Hyde Park, NY. www.newcitypress.com. Used with permission.

Saint Peter Julian Eymard - "Inexhaustible Love" taken from *The Real Presence: Eucharistic Meditations.* © Emmanuel Publications, Cleveland, OH. All rights reserved. Used with permission.

Saint Angela of Foligno - "Contemplating the Sacred Mysteries" taken from *Angela of Foligno: Complete Works (CWS)*, translated and introduced by Paul Lachance, O.F.M. Copyright © 1993 by Paul Lachance, O.F.M. Paulist Press, Inc., New York/Mahwah, NJ. www.paulistpress.com. Used with permission.

Father John Tauler, O.P. - "Our Brother, Our Food" taken from *Spiritual Conferences*, Eric Colledge and Sister M. Jane, O.P., Ed. and Tr. © 1978 by TAN Books, Charlotte, NC (www.tanbooks.com). Used with permission.

Cardinal Robert Sarah - "The Silence of Eternity" taken from *The Power of Silence: Against the Dictatorship of Noise.* Michael J. Miller, Tr. © 2017, Ignatius Press, San Francisco, CA. www.ignatius.com. Used with permission.

Fr. Reginald Garrigou-Lagrange, O.P. - "The Eucharistic Heart of Jesus" taken from *Our Savior and His Love For Us*, A. Bouchard, Tr. Published by B. Herder Book Co., 1951. St. Louis, MO. All rights reserved.

Servant of God Catherine de Hueck Doherty - "Seeing, Believing, Listening, Loving" taken from *Donkey Bells, Advent and Christmas*, Mary Bazzett, Ed. © 1994, Madonna House Publications, Combermere, Ontario, Canada. www.madonnahouse.org

Saint Teresa of Ávila - "Hidden Grandeur" taken from *The Prayers of Teresa of Ávila*, Thomas Alvarez, O.C.D., Ed. Copyright © The Carmelite Nuns of Boston, Boston, MA. www.carmelitesofboston.org. All rights reserved.

Saint Symeon the New Theologian - "Immortal Food" taken from *Symeon The New Theologian: The Discourses.* Translated by C. J. deCatanzaro. Copyright © 1980 by The Missionary Society of St. Paul the Apostle in the State of New York. Paulist Press, Inc., New York/Mahwah, NJ. www.paulistpress.com. Used with permission.

**Father Jean-Pierre de Caussade, s.j.** - **"Faith to See Beyond Appearances"** taken from *Abandonment to Divine Providence*, John Beevers, Tr. © 1975, Image Books, Doubleday & Company, Inc., a division of Random House, Inc. All rights reserved.

**Saint Pius of Pietrelcina** - **"Yes, Jesus, I Love You"** taken from *Letters, Vol. I: Correspondence with His Spiritual Directors*, Fr. Gerardo Di Flumeri, o.f.m. Cap., Ed. © 1984, Our Lady of Grace Capuchin Friary, 71013 San Giovanni Rotondo (Foggia), Italy. www.vocedipadrepio.com.

**Saint Teresa of Calcutta** - **"You Are Precious to Jesus"** taken from Mother Teresa's "Varanasi Letter," March 25, 1993. From *The writings of Mother Teresa of Calcutta* © by the Mother Teresa Center, exclusive licensee throughout the world of the Missionaries of Charity for the works of Mother Teresa. Used with permission.

**Servant of God Luis María Martínez** - **"The Holy Spirit and the Eucharist"** taken from *Liturgical Preludes*, Sister Mary Saint Daniel, Tr. © 1961, The Peter Reilly Company, Philadelphia, PA. All rights reserved.

**Saint Catherine of Siena** - **"O Boundless Charity!"** taken from *The Letters of St. Catherine of Siena*, Vol. I, Suzanne Noffke, O.P., Tr. MRTS Vol. 203 (Tempe, AZ, 2001). Copyright Arizona Board of Regents for Arizona State University. Used with permission.

**Prayers and Scripture readings**

Taken from the *Missale Romanum, editio typica tertia* (2011): *Anima Christi, Suscipe*, Prayer to Our Lord Jesus Christ Crucified, The Universal Prayer attributed to Pope Clement XI. Latin text © Libreria Editrice Vaticana, Vatican City State, 2008. The English translations and chants of The Roman Missal © 2010 International Commission on English in the Liturgy Corporation. All rights reserved.

Taken from the *Compendium on the Eucharist* (2016): *Obsecro Te*; Prayer of St. Bonaventure; *O Bone Jesu*; Salutation to Our Lord Jesus Christ; *Salve, Salutaris Victima*; Prayer to our Lord Jesus Christ; *Domine Iesu Christe, qui neminem vis perire*; *Domine Iesu, Noverim Me*; *Adoremus in Aeternum*; *Ave Verum Corpus Natum*; *Iesu, Dulcis Memoria*; *O Salutaris Hostia*; *Pange, Lingua*. English translation of *Compendium Eucharisticum*, copyright © 2016, Libreria Editrice Vaticana, Vatican City State. All rights reserved.

----------------------------------------------------------------

Adoration companion

Publisher: Pierre-Marie Dumont
Associate Publisher: Romain Lizé
Editor-in-Chief: Rev. Sebastian White, o.p.
Assistant to the Editor: Samuel Wigutow
Layout & Coordinator: Solange Bosdevesy
Permissions Coordinator: Diaga Seck-Rauch
Iconography: Isabelle Mascaras
Cover: Solange Bosdevesy
Translator: Janet Chevrier

Printed by: C.H. Beck, Germany. Edition Number: MGN20037.

NOTES

# NOTES

# NOTES

# NOTES

# NOTES

## NOTES

# And Now...

Are you looking for a trusted resource that can help you grow in your spiritual life, lead you to a more fervent participation at Mass, and offer rock-solid faith formation?

It is all in each issue of MAGNIFICAT!

MAGNIFICAT encourages liturgical, personal, and family prayer. Inspired by the Liturgy of the Hours, this powerful monthly spiritual companion combines the elements of a daily missalette and a monthly magazine.

Prayers for the Morning, Evening, and Night and official Mass texts make it easy for you to begin and end your day in prayer. Superb liturgical insights enrich your experience of the Mass. A daily meditation on the Gospel introduces you to the writings of ancient and modern spiritual masters. Profiles of saints, inspiring articles, lectio divina, art commentaries, and much more invite you into a deeper relationship with Jesus, his Blessed Mother, and his Church.

MAGNIFICAT's convenient pocket size allows you to pray at home, at Church, or wherever you might find yourself during the day with a moment or two for reflection.

Join with hundreds of thousands of Catholics all over the world already reading and praying with MAGNIFICAT every day.

Visit www.magnificat.com and subscribe today.

# MAGNIFICAT®

*Bringing the Word of God to Life*

Each monthly issue is filled with inspirational tools to help deepen your relationship with Jesus, his Blessed Mother, and his Church.

## EVERY DAY, THE TREASURES OF THE CHURCH:

### The Treasures of Prayer

- Morning, evening, and night prayers inspired by the Liturgy of the Hours and adapted to your busy schedule
- First-rate spiritual and biblical essays

### The Treasures of the Eucharist

- Readings and prayers of each daily Mass
- Liturgical insights

### The Treasures of the Saints

- Every day, the inspirational life of a saint, providing a model for daily living

### The Treasures of Spiritual Life

- Carefully selected daily meditations drawn from the writings of the Fathers of the Church as well as from recent spiritual masters

### The Treasures of Sacred Art

- Inspiring, award-winning covers to help your meditation
- Full-color reproductions of great works of sacred art, complete with commentary

# MAGNIFICAT®

*If you liked the Magnificat Adoration Companion,
subscribe to Magnificat for daily support
in your spiritual life!*

| REGULAR EDITION (4.5 x 6.75 in.) | | | | |
|---|---|---|---|---|
| | 6 MONTHS | 1 YEAR | 2 YEARS | 4 YEARS |
| USA | ❑ $26 | ❑ $47 | ❑ $84 | ❑ $149 |
| | or $4.33 a month | or $3.92 a month | or $3.50 a month | or $3.10 a month |

| LARGE PRINT EDITION (5 x 7.75 in.) – 30% larger | | | | |
|---|---|---|---|---|
| | 6 MONTHS | 1 YEAR | 2 YEARS | 4 YEARS |
| USA | ❑ $34.95 | ❑ $64.95 | ❑ $119 | ❑ $236 |
| | or $5.83 a month | or $5.41 a month | or $4.96 a month | or $4.92 a month |

| | REGULAR EDITION | LARGE PRINT EDITION |
|---|---|---|
| CANADA | ❑ 1 year US $54 | ❑ 1 year US $69.95 |
| | ❑ 2 years US $99 | ❑ 2 years US $129 |

For our other English edition (UK, Ireland, Australia), please visit www.magnificat.com

MAGNIFICAT subscribers also have free access to our online and App editions.

**A subscription to the US edition of MAGNIFICAT offers
13 issues a year (one per month and a special issue for Holy Week).
This edition uses the official New American Bible Lectionary.**

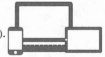

*Please allow 4-6 weeks
from receipt of order for delivery
of your first issue.*

Rates valid until

December 31, 2021.

PLEASE RETURN THIS SUBSCRIPTION FORM TO
**MAGNIFICAT**
**PO Box 822 – Yonkers, NY 10702**

**or call (866) 273-5215
or fax (914) 969-6446
or visit www.magnificat.com**

MAGNIFICAT is also available in Spanish: please visit www.magnificat.com

# MY INFORMATION

TITLE      FIRST NAME

LAST NAME

ADDRESS

ADDRESS

CITY      STATE

ZIP      COUNTRY

PHONE NUMBER      YEAR OF BIRTH

EMAIL

ADOCOMP

# METHOD OF PAYMENT

❏ CHECK ENCLOSED (CHECK PAYABLE TO MAGNIFICAT, US $ ONLY)

❏ PLEASE BILL ME (PARISHES AND INSTITUTIONS ONLY)

❏ VISA     ❏ MASTERCARD     ❏ DISCOVER     ❏ AMEX

CARD No.

EXPIRATION DATE     /     SECURITY CODE

SIGNATURE

**Mailing list:** We occasionally make our list available to other companies whose products or services might interest you. If you would prefer not to be included, please let us know by mail, at **magnificat@magnificat.com**, or by checking this box. ❏

www.magnificat.com